# EFFECTIVE TEACHING PRACTICES

# EFFECTIVE TEACHING PRACTICES
## for
## 21st Century Christian Educators

Revised Edition

Mary E. McConnell, PhD

**Townsend Press**
**Nashville, Tennessee**

Copyright © 2009, 2015 by Mary E. McConnell, PhD
All rights reserved.

Except for the pages that contain a notice granting permission for local church use, reproduction of this work in any form by electronic, mechanical, or other means now known or hereafter invented, including photocopying or recording, or in any information storage and retrieval system, is prohibited without written permission from the publisher. Permission requests may be addressed to Townsend Press, 330 Charlotte Avenue, Nashville, Tennessee 37201-1188; or e-mailed to customercare@sspbnbc.com.

ISBN# 1-932972-15-3

Printed in the USA
Published by Townsend Press
Nashville, Tennessee

# Table of Contents

|  |  |  |
|---|---|---|
|  | Introduction | vii |
| Chapter 1 | Called to the Teaching Ministry | 1 |
| Chapter 2 | The Students You Teach | 8 |
| Chapter 3 | Creating the Learning Environment | 16 |
| Chapter 4 | Learning Styles | 24 |
| Chapter 5 | Lesson Preparation | 32 |
| Chapter 6 | Teaching Methods and Activities | 45 |
| Chapter 7 | Organizing Instruction for Effective Teaching and Learning | 80 |
| Chapter 8 | Teaching and Technology | 105 |
| Chapter 9 | Tips and Tools | 110 |
| Appendix | Training at a Glance | 119 |
|  | Training Outlines | 120 |
|  | Handouts | 131 |
|  | References | 153 |

# Introduction

During the fall of 2007, I presented several weeks of training on "Effective Teaching Practices" to the Christian educators in my church. During the course of the training, I presented information that would be beneficial and helpful not only to the teachers at my church, but also to teachers everywhere who are engaged in teaching God's Word on a systematic basis. Therefore, with God's guidance and inspiration, and having a deep desire and passion to enhance the teaching ministry of the church, I began to formulate my training information and materials into a book format.

Although this book is written with Sunday school teachers in mind, it will also be a most beneficial and helpful resource to superintendents, directors of Christian education, and potential teachers. This book is filled with information on techniques, methods, strategies, and suggestions on how to teach students. Different ways to effectively prepare, plan, and teach a lesson for results are also presented. Throughout the book, teachers are reminded of the importance of their role. Reading, absorbing, and implementing the information in this unique resource will help you improve your teaching skills and abilities—as it is designed to help you become the most effective Christian educator you can be in this post-modern era.

Even if you have been teaching for a long time, you will find this book helpful. The contents in this book will sharpen your teaching skills and help you become even more effective in teaching God's Word. Regardless of the students' ages, you will find this book to be most helpful.

The first chapter is the foundation for the book; it is a discussion of a teacher's calling, commitment, and responsibility to the teaching ministry. The essential criteria and characteristics that Christian educators need to possess in order to be effective teachers in their teaching ministry are covered. Chapter 1 ends by describing the actions of effective teachers.

Chapter 2 points out the importance of establishing teacher and student relationships. Knowing the needs and/or differences of students contributes greatly in your ability to effectively reach, teach, and connect with them. This chapter also presents various ways that teachers can gather information about the students they teach and ways to build relationships.

Chapter 3 provides information on how to create an effective learning environment where all students feel welcomed, supported, and accepted, and where students enjoy studying the Word of God. Ways to assess your classroom environment for improvements are a part of this chapter.

Students learn in different ways. In chapter 4, I present information on learning styles of students and the ways students learn best in each category. Learning through the multiple intelligences is also covered. The importance of knowing how your students learn is emphasized. When we incorporate the different learning-style modalities in our teaching, this allows us to reach and engage all of our students in the lesson. Knowing this information can help teachers develop effective lessons.

In order to teach God's Word effectively, teachers need to be prepared. This preparation can be very extensive. There are certain components that must be involved in the preparation and planning process in order for teaching to be effective. These essential components of lesson preparation are discussed in chapter 5. This chapter is devoted to providing teachers with different lesson preparation tools and resources to assist in their lesson preparation.

Students bring different experiences and different levels of Bible knowledge and understanding to the class and different ways of learning. As a result, it is imperative that Christian educators become familiar with and use different methods of instruction. Different teaching methods and activities teachers can use when teaching a lesson are listed and described in chapter 6. Examples on how to use these methods and factors to consider when selecting a teaching method are presented in this chapter.

How to develop effective lesson plans through a series of systematic steps with lots of examples is presented in chapter 7. In this chapter, I also present information on writing lesson objectives, different ways to introduce the lesson, and teacher assessment measures. This chapter will help you organize and plan lessons effectively; the importance of planning is highlighted in this chapter.

To be relevant and up-to-date, Christian educators must be open to learning about and adapting to technology as a part of their lesson preparation and use. Chapter 8 is an exploration of different types of technology and how it can assist Christian educators in becoming better-equipped and more effective teachers.

A description of some of the most common uses of technology, tools to communicate with your students, and ways technology can enhance your lesson preparation and presentation are some of the areas addressed in this chapter.

Chapter 9, which is the final chapter, provides some simple tips and tools that will add substance and excitement to your teaching and improve your effectiveness as a Christian educator.

Becoming an effective teacher doesn't happen overnight; it is a process of preparation, growth, and development over time. Much of the emphasis in this book is about equipping and preparing Christian educators to be most effective in teaching the Word of God.

***Effective teachers are summarized throughout the book as those who***
- are called to the teaching ministry.
- genuinely care about the students they teach.
- teach with enthusiasm, persuasion, power, and purpose.
- know the students they teach.
- create an environment for learning.
- teach to address the different learning styles.
- use a variety of teaching methods.
- organize instruction.
- develop and use lesson plans.
- teach for results.

After reading this book, it is my sincere prayer and desire that you will be better equipped and prepared and divinely inspired to teach God's Word more effectively.

Enjoy and be blessed!
Mary E. McConnell

# Chapter 1

# Called to the Teaching Ministry

Can you imagine what your church would be like without Sunday school? Or, can you imagine a Sunday school class without a teacher? Teachers are an essential part of the Sunday school teaching ministry. More specifically, trained and equipped teachers who can effectively teach God's Word are vital to the teaching ministry.

In many churches today, Sunday school is the major teaching venue. When you are called to teach a Sunday school class or a Bible study class, you are an integral part of an important and great ministry—the teaching ministry of the church.

Your commitment to the teaching ministry is vitally important to the church. The church cannot function and grow without the teaching of God's Word; studying God's Word is essential to the growth and development of Christians. Without teaching God's Word, churches become stunted in their spiritual growth.

The Sunday school is an established and organized venue for systematic Bible teaching to occur. As a Christian educator, just imagine that you are helping to grow the church spiritually through your teaching.

Being called to the teaching ministry and our ability to teach is a gift from God and a gift to the church. Teachers have a specific purpose and plan to fulfill. God outlined in Ephesians 4:11-13 (KJV) what that specific purpose and plan for teachers is:

"He gave some, apostles; and some, prophets; and some, evangelists; and some, pastors and teachers; For the perfecting of the saints, for the work of the ministry, for the edifying of the body of Christ: Till we all come in the unity of the faith, and of the knowledge of the Son of God, unto a perfect man, unto the measure of the stature of the fullness of Christ."

Furthermore, when you are called to the teaching ministry, you are fulfilling the commandment of Christ, which is to make disciples as He commanded in Matthew 28:19-20 (KJV): "Go ye therefore, and teach all nations, baptizing them in the name of the Father, and of the Son, and of the Holy Ghost: Teaching them to observe all things whatsoever I have commanded you: and, lo, I am with you always, even unto the end of the world. Amen."

## CALLED TO TEACH

I believe Christian educators are called by God to teach His Word.

"God hath set some in the church, first apostles, secondarily prophets, thirdly teachers" (1 Corinthians 12:28, KJV). He is the one who calls, equips, and uses men and women just like you and me to teach and proclaim His Word to others. You have been called, chosen, and commissioned to teach God's Word. As written in 1 Peter 2:9 (KJV), "But ye are a chosen generation, a royal priesthood, an holy nation…that ye should show forth the praises of him who hath called you out of darkness into his marvellous light." What a privilege, an honor, and a blessing! Christian educators are vessels used by God to teach His Word. We are the conduits through which God's Word is taught.

In addition to being called to teach, teachers must have an overwhelming passion and desire to teach. Teaching God's Word should never be entered into lightly; it must be important to you. Christian educators must have zeal, or a drive, a high level of enthusiasm, and an uncontrollable interest and passion to teach.

When embarking upon the teaching ministry, teachers must realize that there is a growing process to teaching. You don't know everything about teaching God's Word when you begin—that is why you must have a desire and a willingness to learn, grow, and develop your teaching skills and ability. To grow and develop your gift of teaching requires study, prayer, and preparation.

As a teacher of God's Word, you have been entrusted with the key that unlocks the door of biblical knowledge of God's Word to share its meanings and messages with people. In other words, you are the communicators, disseminators, and interpreters of the Word of God. As teachers, you are helpers in God's kingdom building.

People cannot grow spiritually and mature in their faith without an understanding of the Word of God. They become stunted in their growth and are often referred to as "babes in Christ." For some, to receive and understand God's Word means coming out of darkness into the marvelous light or passing from death into life. It is critical and crucial to the growth and life of a Christian to study and be taught the Word of God on a regular and systematic basis. That makes your job as a Christian educator so vitally important to the body of Christ (the church).

When we fail to eat on a regular basis, our bodies become weak and frail. Our physical bodies need food and nutrients to grow, develop, survive, and be healthy. In the same way, we need spiritual nutrients to grow, develop, survive, and be spiritually healthy. When our students receive God's Word, they receive the spiritual nourishment and essential nutrients needed for spiritual growth to take place. As a result, they begin to grow in their knowledge and understanding of His Word. If we fail to receive spiritual teaching on a regular and consistent basis, we become weak and frail.

As a Christian educator, your assignment is to teach people the Word of God. The source of your teaching is the Bible, which is God's Holy Word. You are teaching to enhance and develop your students' understanding of the Bible as well as helping them to discover God's truths. Your challenge is to equip your students to be doers of the Word and not just hearers only, as noted in James 1:22. When you do this, you are helping people to grow not only spiritually, but also in every area of their lives. You are helping them to mature in their knowledge and understanding of God's Word. For all of this to happen, Christian educators must have a clear understanding of the Bible and they must study and prepare to be effective teaching vessels used by God. You should not only teach with knowledge and understanding, but also with conviction, assurance, and power.

## THERE IS POWER IN TEACHING GOD'S WORD

There is power in the Word of God—amazing power! The Word of God has the power to heal and transform lives. In studying God's Word, your students will find hope, encouragement, deliverance, salvation, peace, power, and so much more. Sadly, people today are perishing because of their lack of knowledge and understanding of God's Word. People need to hear and be taught the Word of God: "Knowledge is power."

Having the knowledge of God's Word places one in a tremendously powerful position. Not only do students need to have knowledge of God's Word, but they also need to be able to apply this knowledge to answer questions such as, "What does it mean in relation to…?"; and "How does it apply to my life?" When these questions are answered, life-changing results occur. As an outcome of our teaching, we want students to be able to apply what they learn to real-life experiences and situations.

When a person truly receives, understands, and abides by the Word of God, lives will be changed. The Word of God changes lives. The power of God changed my life and your life, and can change the lives of your students as well. Yes, there is power in the Word of God—supernatural, transforming power. It is God's desire through the provision He made through His Son Jesus Christ that all come and know Him, accept Him, and experience His marvelous power.

Therefore, as Christian educators, our job is to teach and plant the Word of God in the hearts and lives of the students that we teach in the most effective and efficient way so that they also can come to know Christ for themselves. To do this, you need the power of God in your teaching. The Bible reads in 1 Corinthians 3:6 (KJV), "I have planted, Apollos watered; but God gave the increase." We are to "water" and He will give the increase. The reference of giving increase used in that verse is to God.

In other words, when we use the phrase "when we water," it means that as teachers, it is our job to teach and plant the Word of God in the hearts and minds of people. It is our job to plant the seed. When we teach God's Word, we are planting godly seeds in the lives of our students. But God is the one who blesses and gives "the increase." It is God and the work of the Holy Spirit which work in the lives of people to bring about conviction, transformation, change, newness, and growth.

Because God's Word is true, it is inerrant, infallible, and eternal. It can be life-changing. His Word is eternal and can give hope in the midst of despair. His Word is the same yesterday, today, and forevermore. There is saving power in His Word, which never changes—thus, it can be trusted. God's Word gives strength in weakness, light in darkness, and hope in despair. It can be a bridge over troubled water. It is the source of spiritual, physical, and emotional healing. One teacher said, "The Word of God is like medicine to the soul." It is the Christian's guide, resource, shield, and instructional book. Every answer to life's questions can be found in the Word of God.

## WITH TEACHING GOD'S WORD COMES MUCH RESPONSIBILITY

With the assignment of teaching God's Word comes much responsibility. When one becomes a Christian educator, she or he is accepting the marvelous and mammoth responsibility of teaching God's Word, equipping the saints, and building the body of Christ, which is the church. You are molding and shaping the lives of others through your instruction, your communication of the Word of God, and living by example. When you take on this daunting task—and it is a daunting task—you become "shepherds" over the students you are assigned to teach. Therefore, this responsibility should not be entered into lightly.

## GOD HAS ENTRUSTED YOU WITH HIS HOLY WORD

God has entrusted His Holy Word to teachers. Can He trust you with His Word? As a Christian educator, you literally have the spiritual lives of the students you teach in your hands. What you say to your students as well as what you do through your actions can have either a positive or negative effect on the decisions and choices they make. It can be a matter of life (eternal) or death (eternal separation). This is one of the reasons why teaching God's Word should be taken very seriously. It should be entered into carefully and prayerfully, with much thought and consideration. Consider James 3:1 (NIV): "Not many of you should presume to be teachers, my brothers, because you know that we who teach will be judged more strictly." The Word must be handled with care.

## TEACHERS AFFECT LIVES

Teachers have a powerful, long-lasting influence on their students, which is noted by Stronge (2002). How are you affecting the lives of those you teach? The writer Hall wrote, in the book *How to Be the Best Christian Educator You Can Be,* that "We teach some by what we say. We teach more by what we do. We teach most by what we are" (Hall, 1986, p. 21). Not only are your students hearing what you are saying, but they are also watching what you say, what you do, and how you do it, in addition to how you respond to life's situations. Therefore, our lives must support what we say.

You may never know the impact and influence you have on the lives of the students you teach. Whether you know it or not, as a teacher, you are making a lasting impression on the students you teach. That is why you should strive to be the best and most effective teacher of God's Word you can be because you are making a difference in the lives of your students. You should do everything possible to make it a positive experience.

## TEACHING REQUIRES A HIGHER LEVEL OF COMMITMENT

When you become a Christian educator, you take on a higher level of commitment. You are expected to do more, and more is expected of you. You are making a commitment to study, learn, and make the necessary preparation to teach God's Word! To do so, you are committing your time, talents, and, in many instances, even some of your resources. You are making a commitment to invest in the lives of the students you teach, which often extends beyond the classroom.

Making such a commitment may require some changes on your part, including revisiting and reassessing your priorities while making some changes and adjustments. As you reflect on your priorities, think about what matters most to you.

To be equipped for this level of service requires preparation and study—from 2 Timothy 3:16-17 (NAS) we learn that "All scripture is inspired by God and profitable for teaching, for reproof, for correction, for training in righteousness; that the man of God may be adequate, equipped for every good work." You cannot successfully teach God's Word to others if you don't know who He is and if you haven't experienced His transforming power and grace in your own life.

In order to be an effective and successful Christian educator, you must know something about the one you teach about—you can't teach what you don't know. That is why it is vitally essential to your growth as a Christian educator to keep learning, studying, and developing your knowledge and skills.

Your job is to provide your students with biblical truths that will equip and empower them to live victorious lives through Christ. You want to teach for change and empowerment in the lives of your students as you create a hunger and thirst for the Word of God in their lives.

Let me share some things I believe teachers of God's Word need to know without doubt or reservation.

- God is sovereign, meaning He is omniscient, all-knowing, and all-powerful. Teachers of God's Word need to know about the sovereignty of God.
- God's Word is true.
- God created the heavens and the earth.
- Jesus was born of a virgin.
- Jesus is the Son of God.
- Jesus died on the cross and rose on the third day.

- It is no secret what God can do. What He's done for others, He will do for you.
- God's Word changes and transforms lives.
- God will hear the cries and voices of *His people,* who believe without question (see Psalm 116). John 3:16 reads, "For God so loved the world, that he gave his only begotten Son, that whosoever believeth in him should not perish, but have everlasting life" (KJV).
- Jesus saves.
- There is no limit to what God can do.

How can you share what you do not have? How can you give away what you don't have? And how can you teach what you don't know? Thus, it is vital to know this and other basic information about biblical beliefs.

## COMMUNICATORS OF GOD'S WORD

Your students must receive your teaching with clarity and understanding. In order to communicate God's Word effectively to your students, you must be knowledgeable of the content you are teaching and you must allow students the opportunity to engage in the communication process. To be effective, both the student and the teacher must engage in the process. If students do not receive what you are saying, effective communication has not taken place. If students do not engage in the communication process, then effective communication has not occurred.

## TEACHING CRITERIA

There are some essential criteria that teachers must possess to be effective teachers. Teachers must have genuine and unconditional love, concern, and care for the students they teach. They must have a desire to teach God's Word. I heard someone say many years ago that Christian educators should "learn it," "love it," and "live it." Teachers must also have the right motives for teaching. Every teacher should examine and understand their motives for teaching. This should be addressed before determining what a teacher is or should be (McDaniel & Richards, 1976). These authors further stated that what motivates someone to teach will clearly have an effect on what kind of teaching he or she does. What are your motives for teaching?

The following are what I consider essential criteria and characteristics that Christian educators need to possess.

**They must**
1. be born-again, having a personal experience of faith in Jesus Christ.
2. have a clear commitment to Jesus Christ.
3. be supportive and committed members of the church they attend.
4. have a vital sense of personal calling.
5. have a clear understanding of the Gospel message.
6. have a good understanding of the Scripture.
7. have a desire to teach God's Word.
8. have the ability to teach.
9. be able to work with people.
10. have a passion for the work.

11. possess an avid love for learning.
12. be teachable.
13. have a willingness to grow and develop teaching talents and skills.
14. have an ability to communicate.
15. have respect for individual differences and learning styles.
16. be enthusiastic about teaching God's Word.
17. have the ability to get along with others.
18. have a willingness and desire to learn more about the Word of God.

As we discuss what is involved in becoming an effective teacher, it is of the utmost importance that you have an authentic testimony that reflects your knowledge, understanding, and personal experience of who God is. Essential areas associated with becoming an effective teacher as well as the necessary tools needed to help you are addressed and presented in the subsequent chapters.

## EFFECTIVE TEACHERS

- Interact with their students.
- Build relationships with their students. It is important to build and establish relationships with the students you teach.
- Build a relationship of love, trust, and encouragement that is demonstrated and felt by the students they teach. Your students should know and feel without any reservations that you care about them.
- Show care for their students inside and outside of the class.
- Are good observers. They observe their students' body language, expressions, and reactions, and make mental notes of what they observe.
- Are good listeners. They listen attentively to what their students are saying as well as what they are not saying.
- Know the students they teach.
- Study.
- Prepare, plan, teach, and evaluate.
- Use a variety of methods and techniques to teach God's Word.

This is a summary list of essential characteristics I believe are also necessary for teachers to possess—"Twenty BEs for Christian Educators."

## TWENTY BEs FOR CHRISTIAN EDUCATORS

**BE** committed
**BE** prayerful
**BE** an example
**BE** a leader
**BE** prepared
**BE** available
**BE** loving
**BE** caring

**BE** concerned
**BE** enthusiastic
**BE** a good listener/communicator
**BE** flexible
**BE** an encourager
**BE** patient
**BE** punctual
**BE** positive
**BE** creative
**BE** a learner
**BE** knowledgeable
**BE** supportive

## POINTS FOR DISCUSSION

1. Discuss the importance of your role as a Christian educator.

2. What do you consider to be the most important criteria Sunday school teachers should meet and why?

3. How should you handle the Word of God?

4. One of your goals should be to become the most effective Sunday school teacher you can be. What are some of the things effective teachers do to achieve this goal?

5. There is power in teaching God's Word. How would you describe this power to your students?

6. Discuss why commitment is important to this work.

7. Assess and reflect on your motives for becoming a Sunday school teacher.

# Chapter 2

# The Students You Teach

How well do you know the students you teach? In order to most effectively reach and teach your students, you must know something about them. When you are assigned to teach a class, whether you realize it or not, you become a shepherd of your students—and a good shepherd knows his or her sheep.

Take time to learn about your students. Failure to know your students limits your ability to effectively reach, teach, and connect with them. Your teaching is more effective when you learn about your students.

## BUILD RELATIONSHIPS

Building and establishing positive relationships with your students is an important part of your teaching ministry. Positive teacher-student relationships are important and do make a difference. Students do better in classes where they experience positive relationships with their teachers.

Establishing positive teacher-student relationships is just as important in Christian education. When you can relate to and connect with your students in a positive way, you will inevitably build relationships. Christian educators must be warm, friendly, and cordial in their expressions.

There are many different ways you can build relationships with your students. One way is to simply let them know that you genuinely care about them and that you accept them for who they are—regardless of where they are in life and where they may be in their spiritual development. "If we want to make a difference, we must show genuine concern for our students. If they perceive that we care, our lessons will find an important spot in their memory banks so that our teaching continues long after the class is over" (Schimmels, 1999, p. 57). According to Hall (1986), "Successful ministry teachers know and care about each student, teaching individuals, not just classes" (p. 21).

Another way to build relationships with your students is to let them know that you are interested in them as individuals and that you genuinely are concerned about them as people. Engaging in conversation with your students and listening to and respecting what they have to say is another way to build relationships. When you do this, you are demonstrating that you value them as people and that you are willing to listen to what they have to say. Exhibiting unconditional love for your students is another way to build relationships. Students remember those teachers who show a special interest in and care for them.

Greeting your students by name is a powerful way to establish relationships. Always refer to each student by his or her correct name, pronouncing it correctly. Treating your students with the highest level of respect also builds relationships.

## WAYS TO FIND OUT ABOUT THE STUDENTS YOU TEACH

Teachers must get to know their students. There are many ways you can gather information about your students. For example, you can learn about the students through the following:

1. Formal or informal parent interviews/conversations
2. Checklists
3. Surveys
4. Questionnaires
5. Student interviews
6. Class activities/presentations
7. Class discussions
8. Games
9. Reflection sheets
10. Observation
11. Assessment of student learning styles
12. Questions

***The following questions can help you as you gather information and learn about the students you teach.***
1. What are their needs?
2. What are their experiences?
3. What do they do?
4. What do they like to do?
5. What are their strengths and weaknesses?
6. What are their expectations?
7. What is their level of understanding about Bible truths?
8. What are their learning styles, or how do they learn best?

Additionally, it is important to find out where your students are in their spiritual level and development. You want to assess and know their level of understanding and knowledge of the Scriptures. Do they know a lot about the Scriptures or do they know very little?

## WHY IS THIS INFORMATION HELPFUL?

Utilizing the information from questions such as those above will assist you in planning and preparing your lessons. It will also help you effectively address the needs of the students you teach. As mentioned earlier, the more information you have about the students you teach, the better you are able to address their needs. This information will also be helpful to you as you seek ways to utilize the skills, the strengths, and the many talents and gifts of the students in your class. You may never know the gifts, talents, and abilities that your students possess if you don't inquire.

The sample survey on page 10 can be used to gather information about your students. The survey on page 11 is designed to be used specifically with children.

Be interested in and concerned about the students you teach. If they miss class, call them, mail a card, or visit them. Let them know that you genuinely missed them in class. Remember that Christian education is more than a classroom commitment.

# Student Survey

Name:_____    Date:_____

1. What do you enjoy doing during your spare time?

2. List your favorite books.

3. What do you enjoy most about attending Sunday school?

4. What are your hobbies?

5. What are some things you dislike?

6. It bothers you when people…

7. What do you do when you find yourself in stressful situations?

8. What are your favorite foods?

9. Are you allergic to anything?

10. What are some of your strengths?

11. What is important to you?

# All About Me

**Place Student's Picture Here**

Name _____

Age _____

What I Like _____

My School _____

Social Activities _____

School Activities _____

Sports _____

Church _____

Family _____

Favorite Bible Verse _____

Accomplishments _____

Awards _____

In addition to learning about the students you teach, it is worthwhile to provide opportunities for your students to learn about each other. There are many ways to bring students together to share and build camaraderie. One way is to put together a classroom scrapbook. You can develop a sheet for the scrapbook (be creative) such as the one below to list specific information about the students in your class. Student scrapbook pages could include the following:

1. Name
2. Birthday
3. School or employment
4. Interests and hobbies
5. Travels
6. Church organizations
7. Family members/children
8. Special talents/achievements
9. Other activities

It is a good idea to attach a recent picture. Another option is to take pictures before or after class. Have your students design and decorate their scrapbook pages. They can then be placed in an actual scrapbook or posted on the walls in your classroom. The scrapbook idea can be tailored for adults as well.

## STUDENT DIFFERENCES

No two people are exactly alike. Students grow, learn, and mature at different rates and levels. We are "fearfully and wonderfully made" (see Psalm 139:14). God made each of us as a different and unique individual. But despite individuality and distinct differences among people, there are many similarities. For instance, people have the need for love, acceptance, belonging, food, shelter, protection, security, and survival. Other similarities may include: enjoying similar activities, the same types of food, and shared experiences.

Just as the students you teach bring many similarities to the classroom, they also bring their differences. Teachers must recognize and respect these differences. Teachers need to know that students bring to the classroom their own

1. ideas
2. values and beliefs
3. opinions
4. likes
5. dislikes
6. cultures/traditions
7. attitudes
8. motivations
9. strengths
10. weaknesses
11. fears

12. prior knowledge
13. experiences
14. skills
15. interests

Additionally, students bring their hurts, pains, disappointments, frustrations, and failures to the classroom. Students grow, develop, and mature at different rates not only physically but spiritually as well. Teachers need to be sensitive to and aware of the differences in the students they teach.

## AGE-GROUP DIFFERENCES

Not only are there individual differences that teachers need to be knowledgeable of, but there are also distinct age-group differences. Become familiar with and learn as much as you can about the age-group characteristics of the students you teach. The following is a brief summary of student age-group social, cognitive, behavioral, and developmental characteristics. Think of the characteristics listed in terms of the students you teach.

### Five- to Seven-year-olds

Typically, children in this age group
- enjoy venturing out.
- have short attention spans.
- have a need for approval from both adults and peers.
- are seeking independence.
- are very imaginative and involved in fantasy.
- find it important to be first and win.
- have an intense eagerness to learn.
- are very active.
- like to talk.
- ask lots of questions.
- have limited concept of time and space.
- are still learning to read.
- may reverse printed letters.
- are eager to learn.
- (girls) are generally ahead of boys in conversational skills.
- have difficulty sitting still for long periods of time.

### Eight- to Ten-year-olds

Typically, children in this age group
- want more independence.
- find it important to fit in and belong.
- are less dependent upon adults.

- have lots of questions.
- are eager to answer questions.
- have high creativity.
- have widening interests.
- can plan and carry out projects with adult support.
- sometimes use words without understanding their meanings.
- are active.
- are curious.

## Eleven- to Thirteen-year-olds

Typically, children in this age group
- have their own opinions and can begin to see more than one side of an issue.
- are very verbal.
- are able to express ideas and feelings.
- enjoy testing limits.
- may exhibit a "know-it-all" attitude.
- experience physical and hormonal changes.
- begin to form individual views.
- want to be independent.

## Fourteen- to Seventeen-year-olds

Typically, kids in this age group
- want to be liked by friends.
- want to be independent.
- are self-conscious.
- undergo physical and emotional changes.
- are sensitive about their appearance.
- have a strong desire for acceptance.
- are becoming more abstract in their thinking.

## ADULT LEARNERS—UNDERSTANDING HOW ADULTS LEARN BEST

To be effective in teaching adults, teachers must understand how adults learn best. Adults have different needs as compared to children. Adults have more experiences to bring to the classroom than children.

Lieb (2008) noted that adults learn best when certain variables are in place. For instance, he noted that adults learn best when
- they feel in control and have choices in the direction of the learning process.
- they are given a high level of respect for their current viewpoints and status.
- there is no condescension by the teacher.
- the teaching builds on their previous experience.

- there is "transferability"—they can apply the teaching immediately to real situations in their own lives.
- teachers realize that most people have a surprisingly short attention span. The hour-long lecture is not, in general, a good means of communication. After about ten minutes of continuous input, people cease to absorb much new information.
- there is a mixture of teaching approaches, including considerable interactivity: role-play or drama, discussion groups, questionnaires, or other feedback.
- visual aids are used—for example: videoclips, graphics, and PowerPoint.
- learners are given the space to come to their own conclusions based on evidence offered to them, in a non-pressured way.
- the learning environment is friendly, informal, and often humorous.
- they have the option to ask questions without fear of embarrassment or condemnation.
- they have a good trusting relationship with the teacher. Learners are looking to see if the teacher's own life reflects the content and usefulness of the teaching: Does he or she "walk the talk"?
- the teaching has a specific, practical, assessable goal, rather than being vague, abstract, or aiming at a range of targets.
- at least some of the learning process is within a small interactive group (Lieb, 2008, p. 1).

Adults also learn through the use of some important instructional tools, as described by Dobrovolny (2003). These tools include the use of reflection, use of prior knowledge and experiences, and use of conversation and discussion skills. As with any other age group, adults need to be shown respect and provided opportunities to express themselves.

## **POINTS FOR DISCUSSION**

1. Why is it important to know something about the students you teach?

2. Why is it necessary to be aware of the differences among the students you teach?

3. What kinds of information would be helpful to know about the students you teach?

4. What differences do students bring to the classroom? Please explain.

5. Describe the different ways teachers can gather information about the students they teach and how this information can be helpful.

6. Describe some of the ways you can build relationships with the students you teach.

# Chapter 3

# Creating the Learning Environment

As a Christian educator, you perform many roles besides spending time in front of your students. One of your roles is to create a positive environment which is conducive to learning, where your students feel welcomed, supported, and accepted, so that they enjoy studying the Word of God.

The learning environment is the location or space where learning takes place. Your task is to create an environment that fosters spiritual growth and development in the lives of the students you teach. You want to create a classroom that reflects the love of Jesus—a comfortable, inviting classroom where fellowship, bonding relationships, and supports are formed, and where students feel loved and that their teacher cares.

Additionally, you must cultivate a culture in which students want to come, participate, and learn. In other words, make the classroom exciting, inviting, and enjoyable for everyone.

For some students, their Sunday school or Bible school class may become a place of solace and security and may be the only support system they have at the time. Knowing this, Christian educators must work at establishing the best teaching environment possible. Yes, the classroom environment that you create and establish is very important.

To illustrate the importance of this point, think back for a moment on some of your own experiences when you were a student. Can you recall being in a class where you did not feel comfortable, or did not feel like a part of the class? Perhaps you were intimidated and afraid to ask questions for fear of being judged, criticized, ridiculed, or ostracized. How did you feel? Did you want to be there? Probably not.

What was the atmosphere of the classroom like? Now, as you look at the opposite end of the spectrum, what is it about the atmosphere of the classroom that you enjoyed so much? What was it about that particular class or teacher that you enjoyed so much?

## YOUR CLASSROOM IS A LEARNING COMMUNITY

Your classroom is a community of learners who come together on a weekly basis to study the Word of God. Students learn better in supportive learning communities. Create an environment where your students can grow and increase in their spiritual knowledge, understanding, and attitudes about the Word of God, and where positive and lasting changes in their lives can occur.

## AN ENVIRONMENT OF ACCEPTANCE IS VERY IMPORTANT

Work at creating an environment that accepts students for who they are—special, unique individuals made by God. Accept where the students are in their spiritual development, realizing that God can move them from where they are to where they need to be. There is no limit to what God can do. He does marvelous things in the lives of people.

To ensure that you are creating the type of environment we have been discussing, it is a good practice to assess and monitor your classroom environment on a frequent basis. Effective teachers are constantly thinking about ways to improve their classroom environments.

## CHRISTIAN EDUCATORS SET THE TONE FOR THEIR CLASS

In addition to the physical environment, as a Christian educator, you also play a very large, integral part in setting the tone and atmosphere for the class. If you exhibit a high level of enthusiasm and interest, your students will have a high level of enthusiasm and interest as well. Enthusiasm is contagious. If your levels of enthusiasm and interest are low, your students will take on your traits of low enthusiasm and interest. In other words, a classroom takes on the attitude of the teacher. What kind of tone are you setting for your class? Are you creating an environment of love, acceptance, and support?

Effective teachers find ways to move their students in the direction of where God wants them to be. They create environments where students feel comfortable and where they like participating and asking questions. Typically, we are generally drawn to people who are warm, caring, and friendly. If your class does not reflect these characteristics, you need to determine why.

## MOVEMENT IN THE CLASSROOM

Another important factor to consider when looking at your teaching environment is the arrangement of the classroom. Arrange your room in such a way that you can see and have eye contact with all of the students in your class. Organize and position tables and chairs to allow for flexibility and arrange the room so that students can see each other and the teacher.

Students interact more effectively when they can see each other. You want to be able to move about and interact with your students during your teaching. Students also need to have ample room to move about as they participate in various activities. Arrange your classroom so that it allows for student movement and involvement.

## REMOVE THE CLUTTER

Get the junk out of your classroom and remove the clutter. Too much clutter can be distracting, annoying, and distasteful, and can get in the way of teaching. The classroom environment should be neat, clean, and attractive. Make your classroom interesting and appealing with lively and colorful bulletin boards and posters that reflect and reinforce what is being taught and that are reflective of the age group you are teaching. Have your teaching materials and books organized neatly in the room. When you remove the clutter, it frees up space and creates a more positive atmosphere.

## CLASSROOM ASSESSMENT TOOLS

An example of a classroom environmental assessment is shown on pages 19-22. This tool can assist you in your efforts to create a supportive learning environment. It allows you to look at and examine closely different variables related to your current classroom environment and structure.

When assessing your classroom environment, look at more than just the physical components such as the room size, arrangement, lighting, distractions, and so forth. Although these components are important, there are other factors that should be considered when assessing your classroom environment, such as teaching preparation, methods, activities, and the level of student participation and expectations. All of these contribute to the learning environment.

I encourage you to complete the "Classroom Environmental Analysis" on page 20. Identify and then implement any necessary changes to make your classroom environment the most conducive and productive it can be.

As you assess your learning environment, envision what you want your class to become. What do you want your class to look like? What is your vision for your classroom? Just as your church and Sunday school department have a vision, you also, as a Christian educator, should have a purpose, vision, and mission for your class. Since much attention is given to the preparation of the lesson, ample attention must be given to providing a classroom environment where students want to engage in studying the Bible and where students want to be. Do your students enjoy coming to your class?

As you begin to assess your teaching environment, you may find it helpful to stop and answer some key questions such as the ones presented in the "Environmental Classroom Checklist" on page 19. This checklist is a quick way to assess some environmental variables.

# Environmental Classroom Checklist

Class:_____   Date:_____

Teacher(s):_____

|  | YES | NO |
|---|---|---|
| 1. Have you assessed your classroom environment lately? | | |
| 2. Do all of your students feel welcomed and accepted in your class? | | |
| 3. Is your classroom dull, or is it attractive? | | |
| 4. Do your students look forward to coming to your classroom? | | |
| 5. Are their ideas and suggestions welcomed? | | |
| 6. Do they get a chance to participate, or do you do all of the talking? | | |
| 7. Is your room set up in such a way that all students can be engaged in the lesson? | | |
| 8. Are there distractions? | | |
| 9. Is spiritual growth taking place in the lives of your students? | | |
| 10. Have you had new students join your class lately? | | |

# Classroom Environmental Analysis

Teacher(s): _____ Age Group: _____ Class: _____

Classroom Location: _____ Length of Class: _____ No. of Students in Class: _____

| **Classroom Environment** | **Teacher Expectations** |
|---|---|
| Describe your classroom setup and student seating arrangement: | What are your expectations for your students? |
| What is the atmosphere in your classroom like? | Describe what your class participation looks like. |
| Identify distracters: | How do you involve students in the lesson? |
| How many students do you typically have? | Do students have assigned responsibilities? |

## Lesson Delivery

What instructional methods do you typically use?

What does your lesson presentation generally consist of?

What do you do to reach all of the students in your class?

## Materials

What instructional materials do you typically use?

What curriculum do you use?

What supplemental resources do you use when presenting the lesson?

| **Teacher Behaviors** | **Outside Assignments** |
|---|---|
| What do you like about your class?<br><br>Is there anything you would change about the way you conduct your class?<br><br>What is your attitude toward your class? | What types of assignments are given and how often?<br><br>How do the students respond to the assignments given? |

Adapted from McConnell et al. (2000). *Functional behavioral assessment: A systematic process for assessment and intervention in general and special education classrooms.*

## **POINTS FOR DISCUSSION**

1. What are some things you can do to help shape and create a supportive learning environment?

2. What are some hindrances to creating a positive learning environment?

3. Complete the "Classroom Environmental Checklist." What did you find out about your teaching environment? What do you want to do differently?

# Chapter 4

# Learning Styles

In the educational arena, you may hear the phrase "One size doesn't fit all," especially when educators are addressing the learning needs of all students. This principle also applies to Christian education. Students differ in their approaches to learning and learn in different ways. Therefore, Christian educators must recognize and remember that you cannot always do the same thing the same way for all students and expect the same results; no two people are exactly alike. God made us different, and created each of us as unique individuals.

Additionally, not all people learn the same way; people learn, retain, and process information in different ways and through different modalities. Some people learn by seeing, hearing, touching, or doing. The differences or approaches in the way people learn are known as *Learning Styles*. Your learning style involves your senses—such as the ability to hear, see, and touch. Although we are constantly using all of our senses, we tend to learn best using certain ones. Christian educators need to be knowledgeable of the different learning styles and how this principle applies to effective teaching.

According to Prenger (1999), teachers who understand their students' learning styles
- are better able to adapt their teaching methods appropriately and are more likely to motivate and engage students in learning by introducing a variety of appropriate teaching methods into their classes.
- can become more sensitive to the differences students bring to the classroom.
- can design learning experiences that either match, or mismatch, a student's style (p. 15).

As noted by Prenger (1999), "Information about students' learning styles is important to both the teacher and the student" (p. 15). To be effective in our teaching, we must be sensitive, knowledgeable, and cognizant of the different ways students learn.

It is important that teachers utilize various teaching methods and approaches that accommodate different learning styles. When this is done, student attainment and understanding of the lesson increases. Information on different teaching methods is presented in chapter 6.

## TYPES OF LEARNING

There are three major types of learners: *visual*, *auditory*, and *kinesthetic*. The different learning styles are presented on page 25 and described on the following pages along with a list of ways you can incorporate the different learning styles into your teaching.

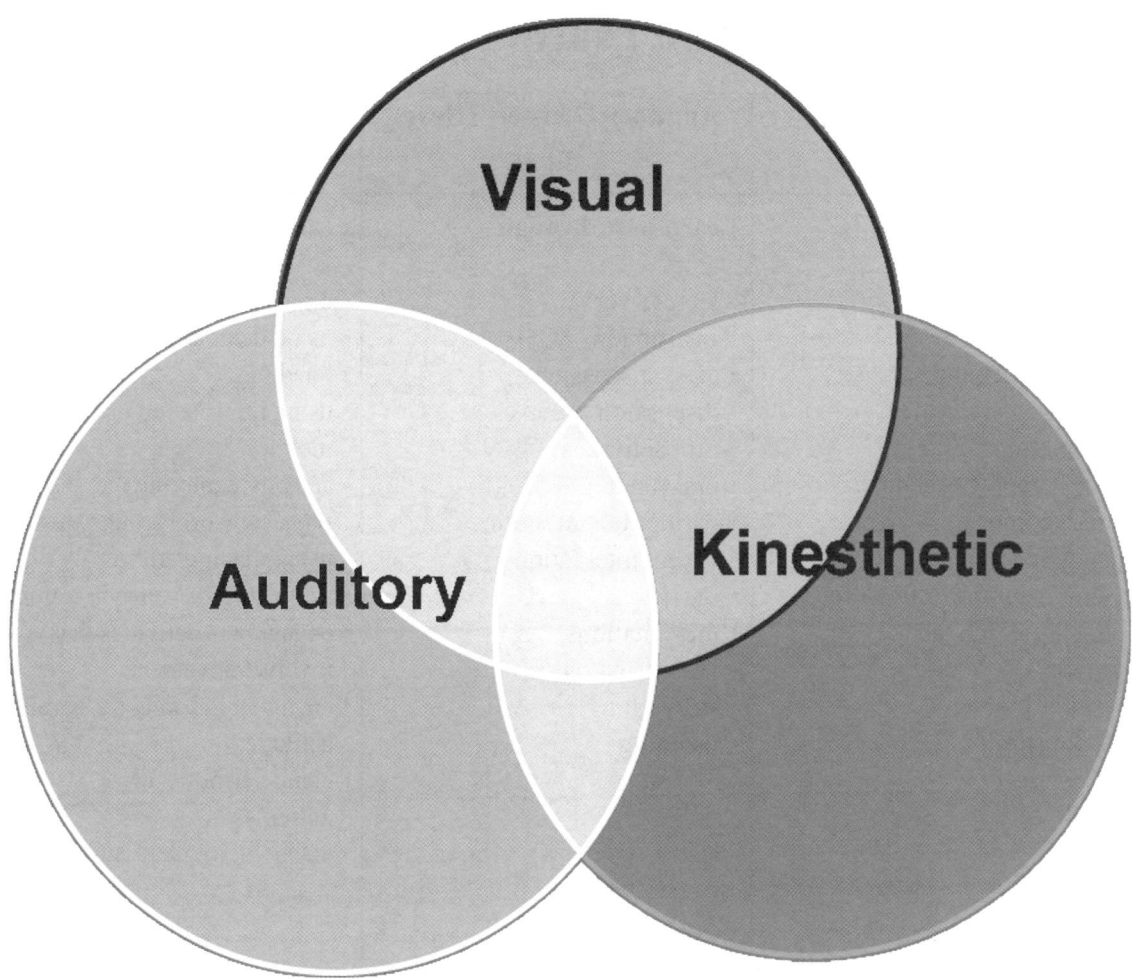

## LEARNING STYLES

### Visual

Visual learners learn best by seeing, watching, and observing things, and have a tendency to remember visual detail (Rief & Heimburge, 1996). Visual learners remember best what they are learning when they can see what it looks like. One way to capture these students' attention is to use colorful charts, dry-erase boards, overheads, and PowerPoint presentations.

### Auditory

These learners learn through hearing and listening. They prefer to hear the instruction presented. Auditory learners are typically very verbal (Rief & Heimburge, 1996). These are generally your talkers.

### Tactile/Kinesthetic

These learners learn best by doing and touching. These are your hands-on learners. They understand better when they are physically involved in what they are learning. They like to be involved in active learning and activities that involve movement.

# Student Learning Styles

| Visual Learners (See) | Auditory Learners (Hear) | Tactile Kinesthetic Learners (Touch/Movement) |
|---|---|---|
| Learn best by<br><br>• reading and reciting from a book<br>• viewing visual displays, images, maps, videos, and pictures<br>• using graphic organizers and mappings<br>• using handouts<br>• using diagrams/illustrations/ charts/pictures/images/ graphs<br>• writing it down<br>• demonstration | Learn best through<br><br>• lecture/verbal instruction<br>• class discussions<br>• discussion groups<br>• oral activities<br>• oral reading<br>• partner talk/activities<br>• verbal interaction<br>• music<br>• presentations<br>• verbal analogies<br>• storytelling<br>• listening | Learn best by<br><br>• direct involvement<br>• using demonstrations<br>• touching<br>• using information that is tied to motion<br>• actively exploring the physical world around them<br>• using manipulatives<br>• actively participating in learning<br>• engaging in activities that involve movement<br>• engaging in hands-on learning activities<br>• using performance activities<br>• engaging in role-plays |

## KNOWING HOW YOU LEARN BEST

Do you know how you learn best? One way to help you determine your preferences of learning is to reflect on lessons taught and then identify teaching methods and activities used. You will probably find that you are teaching in modalities and learning styles that are most comfortable to your learning style preferences.

To reach the students, you must put aside any fears and hesitations that you might have and begin to move beyond your level of comfort, learning to use different methodologies, techniques, and activities that reflect the different learning styles of the students being taught.

When we design lessons to incorporate the different learning styles, we become sensitive to the differences in our students. When we incorporate the different learning-style modalities into our teaching, this allows us to engage all of our students in the lesson. Students are able to comprehend, retain, and understand the lesson being taught when this occurs.

## DETERMINE STYLES OF LEARNING

There are many types of learning style inventories and assessments available for one to determine his or her preference or style for learning. Pages 27-28 contain examples of a learning-style assessment that I have used and adapted over the years to determine how students learn best.

# Learning Style Inventory

Name_____          Date_____

How do you learn best? This inventory helps you determine your learning style. Circle the numbers below that identify how you prefer to learn.

When learning, I prefer to
1. work with my hands.
2. talk to myself while reading a book.
3. hear things explained first.
4. move about and take frequent breaks.
5. watch a DVD or film.
6. experience it.
7. listen to a teacher's or someone's explanation.
8. listen to CDs, tapes, the radio, or recordings.
9. watch someone illustrate or demonstrate the information.
10. perform through simulations, games, or role-plays.
11. look at charts, maps, graphs, or pictures.

When studying something to remember it (memorization), I prefer to
12. say it to myself.
13. write it.
14. read it.
15. hear it.
16. do an activity to learn it.

When reading, I prefer to
17. underline, highlight, or circle important points and write notes in the margins.

Refer to the next page to determine your learning style.

# What Is Your Learning Style?

Place in the identified column the number preferences you circled identifying how you prefer to learn best. Then total the number of circles for each category. Based on the totals, determine your learning style preference.

| Auditory Learners | Visual Learners | Tactile/Kinesthetic Learners |
|---|---|---|
|  |  |  |
| Total | Total | Total |

Based on this learning-style assessment, I tend to learn best using the _____ _____ learning-style modality.

## HOWARD GARDNER'S THEORY OF MULTIPLE INTELLIGENCES

Dr. Howard Gardner, a psychologist, developed the theory of multiple intelligences, which describes eight ways people learn and solve problems. In Gardner's book, *Frames of Mind* (1983), he describes his unique philosophy about how students learn and how teachers should teach. The use of multiple intelligences in teaching supports the following ideas:
1. Students learn in a variety of different ways.
2. Lessons should be presented in a variety of ways.
3. It is a way to help all students learn.
4. It is student-centered and student-focused.
5. It increases learning.
6. It promotes comfortable learning environments for all students.

Multiple intelligences expose teachers to a variety of teaching strategies that help students comprehend, retain, learn, and understand lessons better. A description of Dr. Gardner's eight multiple intelligences is listed below. He suggests that people demonstrate ability in one or more of the intelligences listed. Campbell (1994) stated, "In addition to reading, writing, computing, and listening as instructional tools, students can and do learn through images, textures, rhythm, color, model making, role playing, movement, sculpting, painting, designing, and singing" (p. 9).

As you select instructional methods to use, consider the different ways students learn as proposed by the theory of multiple intelligences. The best way to incorporate this concept is to use different learning activities that represent the different intelligences. Try designing your lessons to include at least two to three of these different areas.

# Multiple Intelligences

| Eight Intelligences | Description *(Persons in this category:)* | Teaching Methods |
|---|---|---|
| **Verbal-Linguistic** | • Enjoy reading, writing, listening and discussing<br>• Think logically, analytically, and sequentially<br>• Have a good memory and recall of information | • Storytelling<br>• Discussions<br>• Debates<br>• Reports<br>• Panel<br>• Creative writing and poetry<br>• Word games<br>• Writing activities |
| **Logical-Mathematical** | • Understand cause-and-effect<br>• Are good at finding patterns and sequencing<br>• Enjoy questioning | • Visual and graphic organizers<br>• Illustrations, analogies<br>• Games<br>• Scenarios<br>• Questioning strategies |
| **Visual-Spatial** | • Are good at forming mental images | • Visual and graphic organizers<br>• Charts, maps, puzzles, games<br>• PowerPoint, slides |
| **Bodily-Kinesthetic** | • Want to feel or experience what they learn<br>• Enjoy doing, moving, and acting things out | • Drama, pantomime, skits<br>• Simulations, games<br>• Role-play<br>• Hands-on activities, crafts<br>• Activities that involve movement |

# Multiple Intelligences (cont.)

| Musical-Rhythmic | • Have a highly developed sense of rhythm<br>• Love music | • Choral reading<br>• Use music in teaching<br>• Songs, singing |
|---|---|---|
| Interpersonal | • Work well with others—are team players<br>• Are naturally sociable, friendly, and outgoing<br>• Work well with others<br>• Are sensitive to others | • Discussion activities<br>• Group activities<br>• Partner activities<br>• Service projects<br>• Simulations<br>• Role-play<br>• Group brainstorming activities |
| Intrapersonal | • Usually choose to work on their own<br>• Understand when they can connect what they need to learn to some personal memory<br>• Are in touch with their inner feelings | • Reflection activities<br>• Individual projects<br>• Journaling |
| Naturalist | • Are highly attuned to the natural world<br>• Loves the outdoors | • Discovering<br>• Observing nature<br>• Projects |

From Campbell, Campbell, and Dickinson (1996), and Silver, Strong, and Perini (2000).

The table below shows how learning styles and multiple intelligences are complementary of each other (Winebrenner, 1996).

| Learning Styles | Multiple Intelligences |
|---|---|
| Auditory | Linguistic<br>Logical-Mathematical<br>Interpersonal<br>Intrapersonal<br>Naturalistic |
| Visual | Visual-Spatial<br>Logical-Mathematical<br>Intrapersonal<br>Naturalistic |
| Kinesthetic | Bodily-Kinesthetic<br>Visual-Spatial<br>Musical-Rhythmic<br>Naturalistic |

Which of the multiple intelligences described above fits into your ways of learning?

## POINTS FOR DISCUSSION

1. Identify and briefly describe the three learning styles presented in this chapter.

2. Complete the Learning Style Inventory on pages 27-28.

3. Through which of the learning styles and multiple intelligences do you tend to learn best?

4. How would you incorporate the idea of learning styles and multiple intelligences into your teaching? Give examples.

# Chapter 5

# Lesson Preparation

To teach God's Word effectively with power, understanding, authority, and accuracy, teachers need to be well-prepared. They must be prepared for the task of teaching in such a way that they are able to effectively articulate and provide biblical truths, relational information, sound doctrine, and even spiritual revelation in a meaningful and productive way.

Teachers need to study and prepare themselves so that they can "rightly divide the word of truth" and be that "approved workman" spoken of in the book of 2 Timothy. For this to happen, they must study and learn as much as they can about the Bible and be knowledgeable of the content they are teaching. Christian educators must teach and handle God's Word correctly.

## GOOD TEACHING MATTERS

Being an effective Christian educator should be your top priority. Just as good teaching is important in the classrooms of our schools, good teaching should be a matter of urgency in our Sunday school classrooms. According to VanSciver and VanSciver (2007), good teaching leads to student learning; the spiritual learning they receive changes lives. The lessons you teach should be carefully studied, planned, and organized. The days of going to the classroom ill-prepared are over. How we teach God's Word does matter.

## LESSON PREPARATION TAKES TIME

It takes time to prepare an effective lesson. That is why it is necessary to start early. I recommend that Christian educators spend at least 7-8 hours a week in preparation and planning. Please note that I stated the word *minimum*. The fact is, you should be engaged in lesson preparation activities on a daily basis. Lesson preparation activities can include praying, reading, meditating, referencing, researching, studying, and so forth.

Waiting until the last minute or even the day before to prepare can be very stressful and is almost impossible. When you fail to allow ample preparation time, you are doing a great disservice to your students, to yourself, and most of all to God. If we are going to teach, God expects us to be prepared; He wants our best service.

With the many demands placed on your time every day, you may find it helpful to put together an outline or schedule to stay on track for daily systematic study and preparation. If you don't plan, it may not happen.

The following is a suggested timeline that can be used as a guide to help you plan and structure your lesson preparation time. Note that the timeline begins on Sunday, after the completion of the lesson you just presented.

# Lesson Preparation Timeline

| Sunday | <ul><li>Pray</li><li>Conduct and review self-assessment of the lesson just taught</li><li>Note changes to implement with the next lesson</li><li>Read title for next week's lesson</li><li>Skim and read outline topics and subheadings in the teacher and student books</li><li>Read lesson and background Scripture</li></ul> |
|---|---|
| Monday | <ul><li>Pray</li><li>Read lesson overview and introduction</li><li>Read related Scripture</li></ul> |
| Tuesday | <ul><li>Pray</li><li>Review last week's lesson and make connections to current week's lesson, if applicable</li><li>Read and gather information from commentaries and other reference materials</li></ul> |
| Wednesday | <ul><li>Pray</li><li>Continue reading Scripture and other resources to gather information and understanding of the lesson</li><li>Think about the lesson in relationship to what is going on in the world today and in relationship to your students</li></ul> |
| Thursday | <ul><li>Pray</li><li>Reread lesson Scripture</li><li>Outline lesson</li><li>Identify lesson objectives</li><li>Identify teaching methods and activities</li><li>Develop lesson plan</li></ul> |
| Friday | <ul><li>Pray</li><li>Gather and prepare teaching materials</li><li>Visualize teaching the lesson to your students</li><li>Practice teaching methods and activities</li></ul> |
| Saturday | <ul><li>Pray</li><li>Review lesson/lesson plan/activities</li><li>Practice teaching lesson</li></ul> |

Prayer is listed at the beginning of each activity for the day. The Scripture reads, "In all thy ways acknowledge him, and he shall direct thy paths" (Proverbs 3:6, KJV). Remember, before we begin our study and preparation, we must first seek God's instruction, wisdom, guidance, and help.

## KNOW YOUR CURRICULUM

How well do you know your curriculum? It is important that you become knowledgeable about and well-acquainted with the curriculum you use. Your curriculum should be
1. biblically and doctrinally sound and accurate.
2. teacher- and student-friendly.
3. age-appropriate.
4. organized in such a way that it is easy to follow and implement.

Most curricula provide lessons, teaching suggestions, procedures, and activities that can be used as you present the lesson. They also provide tools to assist with teaching. Most curricula have clearly defined lesson aims and objectives and provide other useful information and resources that can assist you in teaching your lesson.

Many Sunday schools today use the International Sunday School Lesson Series (Committee on the Uniform Series of the National Council of Churches, USA), a uniform series that provides a listing of Bible study lessons for study across a six-year period. The lessons are selected and designed to cover as much of the Bible as possible over a six-year plan. Some Sunday schools write and develop their own curriculum. Regardless of the curriculum you choose, God's Word should be the foundation, core, and main focus of each Sunday school lesson.

## EFFECTIVE TEACHERS PREPARE THEIR LESSONS WITH THEIR STUDENTS IN MIND

As you prepare your lesson, think of the students in your class. It is a good practice to stop, think, and visualize your students and their needs in relationship to each lesson you teach. While visualizing each student in your class, formulate a picture in your mind of what his or her class participation in the lesson is. As you reflect, visualize your students in the context of the lesson. By doing this, you can determine how to best address the needs of each student as well as make any instructional adjustments needed as you prepare your lesson. These steps lead to effective teaching, which leads to positive student outcomes.

As you begin to prepare, look at the lesson passage from the viewpoint of your students and try to see what they would understand, what they would need explained, and what they can apply to their own lives.

We cannot assume that just because some of our students are knowledgeable of and understand a biblical truth that is being taught, that everyone else in class knows that particular truth as well.

## YOU HAVE A STORY TO TELL

As a Christian educator, you have a story to tell, or a message to deliver. This story is about mercy, grace, love, forgiveness, and salvation. The story is about healing and deliverance, making people whole and complete. "This story is about how God can change the lives of people and lift them to higher heights in Jesus Christ" (McConnell, 1998, p. 9). The story is also about restoration, grace, and hope. The story that you tell can change the life of a student forever. The Word of God changes lives. Tell the story with power and conviction. Tell the story until lives are changed.

## EFFECTIVE LESSONS DON'T JUST HAPPEN

According to McDaniel and Richards (1973), "There is no other way to have a worthwhile lesson except through preparation" (p. 80). Certain components must be involved in the preparation and planning process in order for your teaching to be effective.

*They include*
- prayer
- Bible study or reading the Bible
- reading Sunday school lessons, commentaries, and so forth
- probing for biblical truths and understanding
- studying
- meditating
- researching

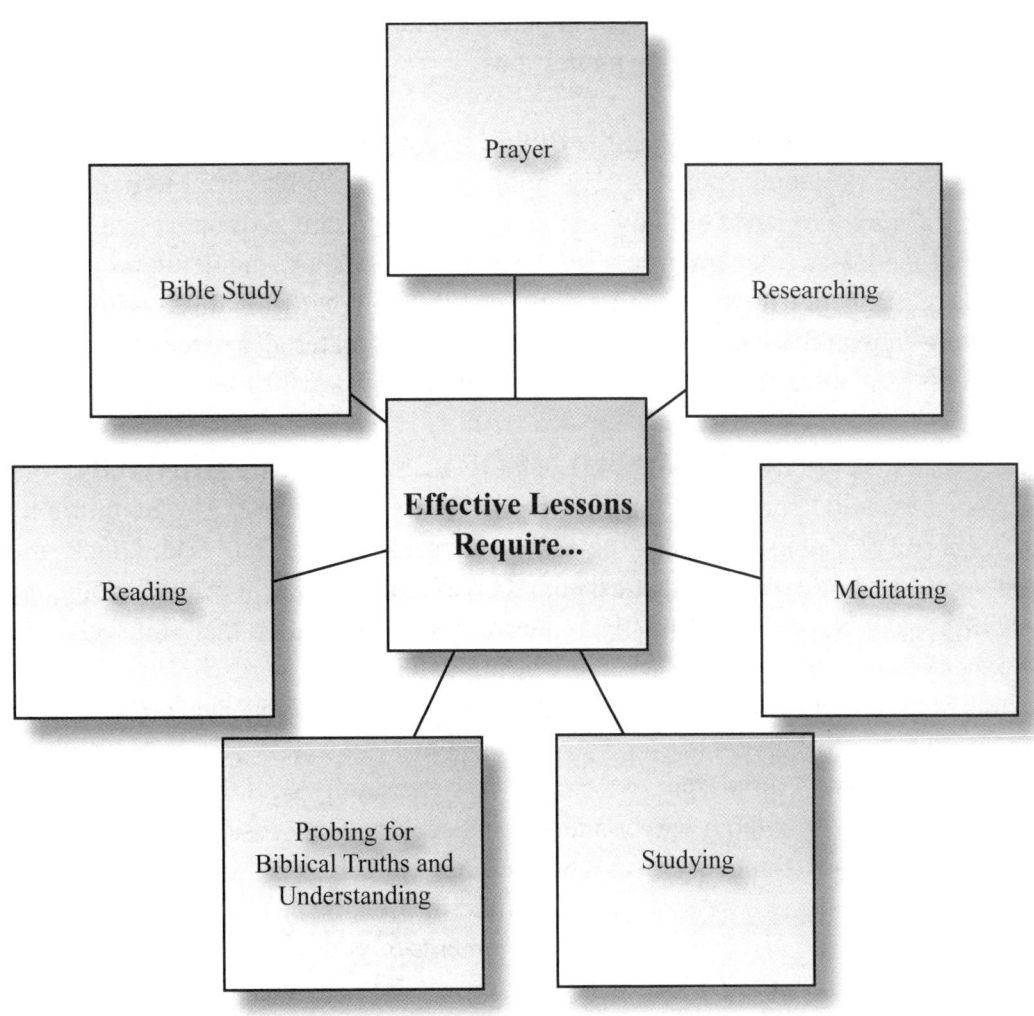

## TEACHER PREPARATION

Before lesson preparation, there needs to be teacher preparation. McDaniel and Richards (1976), in their book, *You and Children*, present an A-B-C-D lesson preparation plan for teaching children. I have adapted and used this plan throughout the years in workshops and trainings with both children and adult Christian educators and have found it to be a very effective blueprint. A description of the ABCD Plan is presented below.

## ABCD TEACHER PREPARATION PLAN

**A.** Ask the Lord to make the lesson real to you. Preparing to teach God's Word should always begin with prayer. Pray and meditate daily. Ask the Lord to give you new understanding, especially of familiar Bible truths. Ask God for wisdom and understanding regarding the Bible portion to be taught. Apply the Bible lesson personally before teaching it to others.

**B.** Begin your study early in the week so the lesson can begin to simmer in your mind. Begin looking at your experiences in relationship to the lesson.

**C.** Concentrate on Bible study. Bible study is digging deeper than reading. Your understanding of Bible truth is the most important part of your lesson preparation. Begin your Bible study with prayer. Use a Bible commentary and other resources for your personal Bible study. Take notes and write down questions.

**D.** Detail your plan. After studying the Bible content, look at your teacher's book. It is your second teaching tool. Your teacher's book should be the blueprint to help you translate your learning into terms, and by methods that your pupils will understand. Follow your teacher's book as a general rule. The ideas in your teacher's book are prepared for thousands of teachers who are teaching children/adults in many locations with very different backgrounds and experiences. Tailor the teaching material to meet the needs of your students. (Adapted from McDaniel & Richards, 1976; p. 80.)

## PRAYER: AN ESSENTIAL COMPONENT OF LESSON PREPARATION

Prayer is an essential component in the lesson-preparation process. The Scripture tells us in Matthew 7:7-8 (KJV), "Ask, and it shall be given you; seek, and ye shall find; knock, and it shall be opened unto you: For every one that asketh receiveth; and he that seeketh findeth; and to him that knocketh it shall be opened." Christian educators, it is imperative that you seek God's guidance in all that you do and especially when preparing to teach His Word.

Do you need more understanding, knowledge, and wisdom in your teaching? If so, ask God for what you need. He will give it to you. David, in Psalm 119:10 (KJV), prayed, "With my whole heart have I sought thee." Simply put, we cannot be successfully equipped to teach God's Word effectively or successfully without prayer and without seeking God. Jesus Himself recognized the importance of prayer in His ministry, as we see in Mark 1:35 (KJV): "And in the morning, rising up a great while before day, he went out, and departed into a solitary place, and there prayed."

Start your day with prayer. Give God the first moments of your day. Begin praying for yourself, then for each of your students, and for the lesson you will be teaching. The saying "Much prayer, much power; little prayer, little power" suggests that the more prayer you engage in, the more power you will have when teaching your lesson. To be effective, you need the power of God in your life. The way to get this power is through prayer.

As you ask the Holy Spirit to unfold the Scriptures to you, pray for wisdom on how to teach the lesson. Pray for revelation and an unfolding of new biblical truths when preparing to teach familiar Bible lessons. Pray for guidance, direction, and purpose. Pray to communicate God's Word powerfully and effectively with each student. Pray for your students' understanding of the Word, open minds, and receptive hearts to receive what you are teaching. In summary, include God in every facet of your preparation, planning, and teaching.

## HOW TO BE BLESSED IN YOUR TEACHING MINISTRY

To be blessed and fruitful in your teaching, you must trust God and acknowledge Him in all that you do in your preparation to teach. Proverbs 3:5-6 (KJV) reads, "Trust in the LORD with all thine heart; and lean not unto thine own understanding. In all thy ways acknowledge him, and he shall direct thy paths." Put your teaching ministry in the hands of God. Seek His counsel and wisdom and make God a vital part of every lesson. Depend upon God totally for guidance and allow the Holy Spirit to motivate every Scripture, theme, and points of the lesson you teach. This is all done for His glory and edification of the body of Christ.

## STUDY TOOLS

To study and prepare an effective lesson requires that you have and use appropriate study tools and resources. Just as a surgeon, a builder, or a hair stylist needs specific tools, equipment, and supplies to do his or her job effectively, it is the same with Christian educators. Not only do they need to be equipped with their essential tools, but they also need to know how to use them. Some of the important tools that every Christian educator should have are these:

1. Study/reference Bible (more than one translation)
2. Concordance
3. Bible dictionary
4. Dictionary/thesaurus
5. Bible handbook
6. Bible commentaries
7. Lesson commentaries
8. Sunday school book (student and teacher)
9. Bible atlas/maps
10. Highlighters/markers (different colors)
11. Notebook/binder
12. Note cards (optional)
13. Study Web sites or biblical software

Be diligent in utilizing these tools, resources, and study helps to assist in your teaching preparations. You can also find a wealth of information on the Internet. It is important that you have accurate facts and information about the lesson you are teaching.

The following pages list lesson preparation tools that I developed for Christian educators to use when studying and gathering information on a lesson. These tools are "Lesson Preparation: Ten Key Questions to Ask"; "Lesson Preparation Organizer: Who, What, When, Where, Why, How"; and "Lesson Preparation Worksheet."

Have these tools on hand as you study and prepare. The Lesson Preparation Organizer presented later in this volume is presented in a graphic organizer format (Graphic Organizers are discussed in detail in chapter 6). This lesson plan organizer asks for similar information that is outlined in the "Lesson Preparation: Ten Key Questions to Ask" form presented on the next page, but in a more simplistic way. Select the format that works best for you.

# Lesson Preparation: Ten Key Questions to Ask

Lesson Title:_____ Date:_____

Lesson Scripture:_____

As you **read, study,** and **prepare** your lesson, ask **Who, What, When, Where, Why,** and **How** questions such as the ones listed below.

1. Who is speaking in this lesson? _____

2. Who is the author speaking to? _____

3. What time period was this lesson written? _____

4. What was going on at the time this lesson was written? _____
   _____
   _____

5. What are the main themes in this lesson? _____
   _____
   _____

6. Why did the author write this lesson? _____
   _____
   _____

7. What is the message in this lesson? _____
   _____
   _____

8. What happened as a result of the message in this lesson? _____
   _____
   _____

9. How does this lesson apply to today? _____
   _____
   _____

10. What does this lesson mean to me? _____
    _____
    _____

# Lesson Preparation Organizer:
## Who, What, When, Where, Why, How

**Lesson Title:** _____  **Date:** _____

| |
|---|
| Who |
| What |
| When |
| Where |
| Why |
| How |

# Lesson Preparation Worksheet

**Lesson Title:**_____ **Date:**_____

---

Additional Scriptures and references to read:

---

Additional reading resources:

---

Key words and terms:

---

Special preparation:

## LESSON OUTLINES

An outline is another way to help you organize your notes, thoughts, and information about the lesson in a systematic and orderly format. An outline can help you frame the presentation and can be developed as you study and prepare. More specifically, having an outline
- helps you structure and organize your ideas, main topics, main points, and subtopics of the lesson.
- presents your material in a logical format.
- groups related ideas and topics together.
- is a way to arrange material in subsections from general to specific or from abstract to concrete.

The following is an example of a lesson outline that was used in the preparation and teaching of a lesson on the prophet Nehemiah.

## Lesson Outline

Lesson: Up Against the Wall
Scripture: Nehemiah 4:1-3, 7-9, 13-15; 6:15

I. Nehemiah continued the Lord's work in the face of opposition

II. Enemies tried to stop the work (verses 1-3).
   A. Working despite ridicule
      1. Sanballat and Tobiah ridiculed the work of God.
         a. They were deeply disturbed when they heard a man wanted to help the people of Jerusalem.
         b. They attempted to discourage the workers.
      2. They mocked Nehemiah and the people.
      3. They tried to stop the Jews from building the wall.
      4. They were angry.
      5. They used scorn and intimidation to prevent the work from starting.
      6. They were furious and very indignant.
      7. Sanballat and Tobiah sought to bring the discouragement through criticism, threats, and bluffs.

III. Instead of returning insults, Nehemiah prayed and the work continued (verses 4-6).
   A. Nehemiah was not praying for revenge but that God's justice would be carried out.
   B. The people continued to work. They did not give up.

IV. The enemies wanted to fight against Jerusalem (verses 7-9).
   A. They wanted to stop the work.
   B. Nehemiah and his helpers prayed to God for help.

V. This was Nehemiah's response to opposition (verses 13-15).
   A. Nehemiah was warned of their plans to attack.
   B. They set a watch against their enemies day and night.

  **1.** They watched and prayed.
  **2.** They prepared themselves for an attack.
 **C.** The men were divided into two forces.
  **1.** One to work.
  **2.** The others stood ready to fight.
  **3.** Nehemiah told them that God would help them fight if they were attacked.

**VI.** The wall was completed (4:14; 6:15).
 **A.** Nehemiah told the people not to be afraid of their enemies.
 **B.** The wall was finished in fifty-two days.

## PRE-PLANNING VARIABLES TO CONSIDER

Teaching an effective lesson begins long before actually teaching the lesson. Ormrod (2000) writes, "Effective teachers engage in a considerable amount of advance planning. They identify the knowledge and skills they want their students to acquire, determine an appropriate sequence in which to foster such knowledge and skills, and develop classroom activities that will promote maximal learning and keep students continually motivated and on task" (p. 518).

Before you begin to study and prepare your lesson, there are some key questions that you should consider. In fact, it may be helpful to have these questions at hand as you engage in the pre-planning process so that you can quickly respond to them as instructional ideas come to you.

The Key Questions to consider are these:
1. What is the lesson aim?
2. What do I want the students to learn and be able to do at the end of the lesson?
3. How will I introduce and close the lesson?
4. What preparation do I need to make for this lesson?
5. How will I teach the lesson to address the learning needs and learning styles of all students?
6. What methods/activities/teaching aids should I consider using?
7. What materials do I need for the lesson?
8. How do I plan to engage students in the lesson?
9. Are there any special accommodations I need to make?

## PRACTICE YOUR LESSON ALOUD

Practicing your lesson before teaching it to your class is a good practice to follow. This is especially important when you are preparing to use a method or activity that you have not previously utilized, or one with which you may not be as familiar. Spend time learning and practicing the method before using it with your students. We are all familiar with the saying, "Practice makes perfect." It is an undeniable truth that the more one does something, the better he or she becomes at it. You can practice in front of a mirror, record your presentation and listen to it, or videotape and view it for a critique—or you may have a built-in audience (family members) you can practice with. Practicing your lesson every week will help build your confidence as it improves your teaching ability.

## **POINTS FOR DISCUSSION**

1. What are some key components that should be a part of your lesson-preparation process? Briefly discuss each component.

2. Why is it important to prepare your lesson with your students in mind?

3. Identify at least eight study tools every Christian educator should use.

4. Describe the ABCD Teacher Preparation Plan outlined in the chapter.

5. Based on a Sunday school lesson you taught recently, complete the Lesson Preparation form on page 39.

6. Discuss three to six pre-planning variables that teachers should consider when they prepare a lesson.

# Chapter 6

# Teaching Methods and Activities

*We learn 20 percent of what we read, 30 percent of what we see, 50 percent of what we both see and hear, 70 percent of what is discussed with others, and 95 percent of what we teach to others.* (William Glasser)

Many Christian educators are still teaching every lesson every week the same way—using the same methods all of the time as if all students learn in the same manner. This is alarming, since students differ in how they learn, process, and retain information. Some students like to hear and discuss, others like to see and visualize, and some just like to experience and do.

If your students can't hear it, see it, say it, do it, or touch it, they may not be learning and receiving the biblical truths that you want to impart. An old adage goes, "Tell me and I forget, show me and I remember, involve me and I understand." The diagram below shows that students learn better when they can do it, say it, and see it, and learn the least when they only hear it.

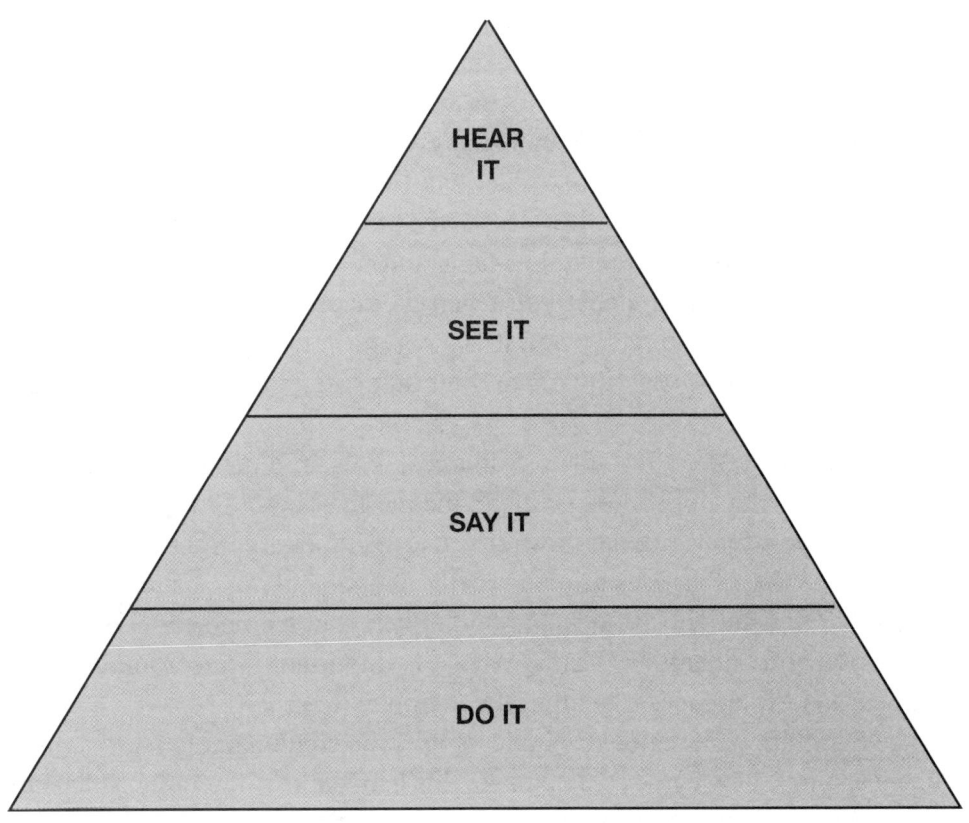

Since students bring different experiences and different levels of Bible knowledge and understanding to the class, it is imperative that Christian educators become familiar with and use different methods of instruction. Teaching methods and activities must accommodate the different ways that students learn. That is why it is so important that you present lessons using the various modalities of learning. When this is done, you have a better chance of reaching all of the students in your class. I challenge you to "step outside the box" and comfort zone and begin to explore and use different methods of instruction.

## TEACHING INVOLVES MORE THAN TELLING

Teaching is more than telling. It involves presenting information, ideas, and concepts. Good teaching stimulates and motivates students to learn and think for themselves. I heard someone define *teaching* this way: "Teaching is creating an experience in which another person changes in some lasting way his or her knowledge, understanding, skill, attitudes, or values through an exchange of information, ideas, and experiences." We want to move our teaching beyond merely teaching and telling, to the point where we are engaging our students through various methods of instruction that involve them in the teaching/learning process that results in change.

Galindo (2006) explains, "Teaching by 'telling' does not change learning, because teaching-by-telling does other people's thinking for them. The power of learning is active and dynamic" (p. 15). In his definition of teaching, Sisemore (1977) defined *teaching* in the context for Christian educators as "the explanation of the gospel primarily to the believer so that he can understand his faith and grow in Christian grace" (p. 41).

Teaching is also more than having students memorize content. "Our purpose in Bible teaching is more than to impart facts; it is more than to drill pupils so that they can quote Scripture verses from memory" (Colson, 1970). Memorizing God's Word alone is not enough. We want to move our students beyond rote memory and facts alone—even though those are important to help them understand and apply the biblical truths they are learning. In order to grow spiritually, students need to do more than just remember facts and information. God's Word must be alive and working in the lives of the students you teach week after week. Furthermore, teaching is more than regurgitating what you have read; it is a carefully thought-out plan of presenting and sharing the information you want to impart to your students in a systematic, orderly, accurate, and purposeful manner.

Effective teachers everywhere use many resources, tools, and methods to help children learn. Your goal as a Christian educator should be to get the message across to your students in the most effective and productive way, using the most effective methods. In order for this to happen, you need to acquire a repertoire of various teaching methods and activities that effectively engage students in the lesson. You want your students to be thinkers and learners, applying and using what they learn to everyday life situations. That is why it is important to incorporate real-life circumstances, situations, and experiences into all of the lessons.

Knowing the Scripture is not enough. Students must be challenged to *understand, use, apply,* and *live out* the teachings they learn. To help make this happen, it will require a change in how you teach. "God desires that beyond mere head knowledge, our hearts would be changed and our lives and actions would be affected by what we learn" (Hull, 2006, p. 89).

## FACTORS TO CONSIDER WHEN SELECTING A METHOD

When selecting teaching methods, consider the following factors. Teaching methods should be

1. meaningful.
2. purposeful—What is the purpose of using the selected method(s)?
3. age-appropriate. (Does the method fit the age group?)
4. applicable to the class and class size.
5. practical.
6. related to the lesson.
7. at the students' level of understanding.

Another factor to consider when selecting a teaching method is the content of the lesson. Different lessons warrant different methods of instruction. Not all lessons should be taught in the exact same way.

## JESUS, OUR EXAMPLE

Much of Jesus' earthly ministry involved teaching. Examine and study the ways Jesus taught. Jesus, the Master Teacher and the greatest teacher ever, used different methods of teaching on different occasions and settings and adapted His teaching to the audience to get His message across. In Jesus' teachings, He used examples that were familiar and related to people. He used parables, analogies, stories, demonstrations, questions, visuals, illustrations, and objects as methods to get His message across to His listeners. For example, Jesus used the metaphor of "living water" when He talked to the woman at the well; "seed" when He talked to farmers; and "nets" and "fishers of men" when He talked to fishermen. To impart God's Word in the most effective way requires that we also use different methods of teaching.

As you prepare your Sunday school lesson, find ways to connect Bible truths with the experiences of your students. That is why it is important to know something about the students you teach.

## MAKING SMOOTH TRANSITIONS

When using more than one method of instruction, it is important that you transition quickly and smoothly from one activity to the next. Your teaching time is valuable. You want to be careful and thoughtful in the use of your time. If you don't plan carefully, valuable class time will be wasted during instructional transitions.

Transition is merely moving from one activity to the next. For smooth transitions to occur, you must be well-acquainted with the instructional activity or method of instruction, have materials ready for the activity, and provide clear and concise instructions to follow. Moving smoothly from one activity to the next requires practice and planning. In order to help make smooth transitions, the following is suggested:

1. Practice the lesson out loud to yourself before teaching it to the class.
2. Work through teaching methods and activities.
3. Practice transitioning between activities with a timer.
4. Make sure students understand what their roles are in the activity.

5. Give clear and explicit directions and instructions to students before making the transition. Make sure all students clearly understand the task at hand. When students receive instruction before transitioning, it makes for a better and smoother transition. For example, if you are going to engage students in a brainstorming activity, give clear instructions, examples, and expectations before they are transitioned. For a group activity, have groups assigned ahead of time so when students make the transition they are fully prepared and ready to begin the task. When teachers plan for transitions, they will avoid losing valuable instructional time.
6. Use established signals for transitions (to begin and end an activity). For example, flashing the lights off and on, using bells, whistles, timers, upbeat songs, visual cues, raising the hand in a "V," and clapping patterns can be used to get the attention of your students.
7. For children, make sure you teach, model, and practice the procedures that will occur when changing activities.
8. Give students a time warning to finish an activity. For example, say, "You have three minutes to finish up."
9. Be organized, prepared, and ready for the next activity.

## TRADITIONAL VERSUS MORE EFFECTIVE METHODS

Traditional methods are good, but they should not be the only methods used today when teaching God's Word. When traditional methods alone are used, this limits your ability to engage all students in the lesson. On page 49, there is a comparison and contrast of "Traditional Methods" versus "More Effective Methods" used by teachers. Which category do you fit into?

## JIGSAW

Jigsaw is a cooperative reading activity that involves group learning and sharing. One example of using this strategy is to assign students to work in groups of three to five people. Each group is given an assigned section to read, learn about, and get familiar with. Group members can decide who and how they are going to read their assigned section. Participants are then instructed to highlight or write down three or four important parts from their sections. Group members discuss the main points from each section read and determine what key information from their reading to share with the whole group. Each part of the passage read by the group is essential for the completion and full understanding of the topic assigned.

## GALLERY WALK

Gallery walk is another interactive learning strategy that gets everyone involved in the learning process. It can be used as an opening, closing, or review activity. A question, quote, statement, idea, or Scripture is posted on large charts of paper around the room. Groups of three to six participants are assigned to each of the charts and are instructed to read, discuss, and comment on what is posted on their chart. Each group is then instructed to move to the next chart and review ideas listed, respond, and add new ideas. Group teams continue this process until they reviewed all the charts whereupon they return to their original chart. Finally, someone from each group summarizes main points of just the original chart to the whole group. This is one activity that gets students up and moving as they are discussing and learning valuable content. Group members are given the opportunity to communicate their ideas as they also listen to their teammates. This is a great activity for youth and adults.

| Traditional Methods | More Effective Methods |
|---|---|
| *The Teacher . . .* | *The Teacher . . .* |
| • Uses lecture only | • Uses different methods of instruction |
| • Teaches each lesson in the same prescribed way | • Plans lessons to address different learning styles |
| • Stands in front of the class | • Moves around the classroom to connect with students |
| • Asks students to read and explain a verse | • Engages students in the lesson |
| • Asks students questions about the lesson | • Has a lesson plan and objectives for each lesson |
| • Expects students to listen and learn | • Encourages students to discover, inquire, explore, ask questions, and participate in discussion and small-group activities |
| • Only writes on the blackboard | • Uses slides, visuals, charts, and so forth |

If you are a teacher using traditional methods that involve lecture only, then it is time to explore and begin to make the paradigm shift to using different methods of instruction. When teachers use a variety of teaching strategies, it contributes to their effectiveness as teachers (Stronge, 2002). Following this, you will find a list of methods and activities that can be used when teaching a lesson. Subsequent to that is a description of some of those methods that are most commonly used.

# Teaching Methods and Activities

| K-W-L Charts | Questions | Group Activities | Games | Group Discussions |
|---|---|---|---|---|
| Pre-Quiz (oral or written) | Brainstorming | Compare-Contrast | Think-Pair-Share | Demonstrations |
| Oral Presentations/Reports | Scenarios | Worksheets | Pictures/Diagrams | Partner Activities |
| Videos/Films/Movies | Analogies | Review of Current Event Related to the Lesson | Simulations | Role-plays |
| Creative Writing/Drawings | Illustrations | Reflection Activities | Storytelling | Graphic Organizers |
| Case Studies | Lecturing | Panel Discussions | Reports | Skits |
| Projects | Class Discussions | Interviews | Drama | Debate |
| Scripture Search | Listening Teams | Post-Quiz (oral or written) | Instructive and Creative Play | Teaching through Music |
| Small-group Activities | Visual Aids | Art Activities | Puppets | Slides/PowerPoint Presentations |
| Buzz Groups | Seminars | Constructive Play | Technology | Music |
| Outlines | Round Robin | Cooperative Learning Games | Pantomime | Slide Presentations |
| Inquiry-based Learning | Inductive Methods | Problem-based Learning | Visual Charts | Questionnaires |

To reach all the students they teach, Christian educators must stretch themselves and move out of their comfort zones. Don't be afraid to use different teaching methods. We want to impart God's Word to our students in the most effective way possible. One way to do this is to involve students in the lesson. Allow your students opportunities to articulate what they think, know, and feel.

## DIFFERENT WAYS TO READ AND PRESENT THE BIBLE PASSAGE

As stated by Hull (2006), "Reading God's Word empowers us for spiritual growth" (p. 120). Reading Scripture passages from the Bible should be a part of every lesson. However, in addition to reading the Scripture text verbatim, there are other ways you can introduce the Bible text. In his book, *How to Be the Best Christian Study Group Leader Ever in the Whole History of the Universe*, Galindo (2006) listed different and creative ways that teachers can read, present, and interpret the biblical text. Some of the ways he suggested include the following:

1. *Read it dramatically*—For example, if your lesson is taken from a Bible story passage that is in story form, have students read the text as a drama.
2. *Act it out*—This can be used with a dramatic text or a Bible story. Students can read from the text or a prepared script, or improvise.

3. *Show it*—This can be done through the use of videos, stories, and passages.
4. *Picture it*—Show the Bible text through art or graphics, even from a flannel board.
5. *Draw it*—Ask students to draw a Bible passage.
6. *Paraphrase it*—Have students put the Bible passage into their own words.
7. *Sing it*—Many of the Bible passages from the Psalms, Lamentations, and Proverbs can be sung.

Gangel (1982) describes teaching methods as processes and techniques that the teacher uses to teach the lesson. The remaining section of this chapter presents various teaching and instructional practices and methods that Christian educators can use when teaching a lesson. Many of the methods presented can be applied to all age levels.

## TEACHING METHODS AND ACTIVITIES
### Lecture
Lecture is probably the teaching method that is used most frequently. The lecture method is generally used to
1. give an overview and introduction of the lesson.
2. present background information.
3. present basic facts and information.
4. define key words and terms.

This method works well for large groups and is appropriate to use when you are presenting a lot of factual information. However, this method limits student participation, especially for children. Using this method of instruction alone limits interaction, activity, and participation from students.

Other methods and activities can be incorporated with the lecture method to make it more interesting. For instance, Gangel (1982) suggests eight ways that teachers can improve their teaching when using the lecture method.

*Teachers can*
1. combine the lecture with audience involvement, such as discussion, reaction groups, or a question-and-answer period. This allows for feedback and gives the lecturer an opportunity to clarify any concepts which might not have been understood by students.
2. support the lecture with visuals such as the chalkboard, overhead projector, or charts.
3. have a clear and simple outline.
4. practice good principles of speaking, such as eye contact, voice inflection, and proper posture.
5. emphasize the important points.
6. use interesting illustrations.
7. specify clear objectives for the lecture (p. 15).

As you can see, there are different ways you can present the lecture method that can add variety and spice to your teaching.

## QUESTIONS
Questions are a wonderful way to engage students in the discussion of the lesson and check for student understanding. Asking the students questions is not only a great way to facilitate

communication between teacher and students, but it is also a way to assess what they know and what they do not know. When asking questions as part of your instructional method, make sure your questions are meaningful and purposeful with intent in mind, well-thought-out, and carefully planned and written ahead of time.

State the question clearly and allow students ample wait time to answer. Research has consistently demonstrated that the quality of student verbal responses improves when teachers regularly use the "wait time" technique. This technique allows students the time after a question is asked to process and develop a response to the question. Ask one question at a time. Don't confuse your students by asking several questions at the same time.

Since we know that people receive and process information differently, it is important that we present questions to our students in more than one modality. For example, questions can be presented to students on an overhead projector, chalkboard, flip chart, or typed on paper as handouts. You can also ask students to paraphrase, or repeat the question orally, to check their understanding of the question—or they can repeat it with a partner.

When asking questions, make sure that all students understand what is asked. Gangel (1982) states, "If a question is not clear to a student, it should be repeated in different verbal forms so that the student can grasp the significance of what is being asked" (p. 41). When it comes to understanding God's Word, there is no room for assumptions. We want to make every part of our teaching clear. As stated, asking questions is one way to check for understanding and to gauge whether students understand the lesson. Asking good questions opens the door for discussion.

## A FRAMEWORK FOR WRITING QUESTIONS

*Bloom's Taxonomy of Educational Objectives*, a system for organizing and developing questions at different levels, can assist the teacher in writing questions. (*Bloom's Taxonomy* is further discussed in the next chapter.) *Bloom's Taxonomy* consists of six levels or categories of question types. They are classified and progress from the lowest level to the highest level—Knowledge, Comprehension, Application, Analysis, Synthesis, and Evaluation—with Knowledge being the lowest level.

Many times, teachers tend to ask questions at the "Knowledge" and "Comprehension" levels which are at the lower level of the system. These questions require little preparation. Questions at these levels typically engage students to recall, define, explain, or summarize what they have learned.

Try not to use these types of questions all of the time. Formulate questions that go beyond a simple knowledge response but rather generate thinking that utilizes the higher order level of questions. Challenge your students to engage in the types of questions that provide opportunities to analyze, compare, and contrast and use higher-level thinking skills. The higher levels of questioning are those at the analysis, synthesis, and evaluation levels. Writing higher-level questions requires more thought and preparation than when you are writing lower-level questions—but it is time well-spent. A table of the different categories listed in *Bloom's Taxonomy* is presented in chapter 7.

## OPEN-ENDED AND CLOSED-ENDED QUESTIONS

An *open-ended* question is one for which there can be many acceptable answers. Higher-order questions tend to be open and encourage students to think more critically. An example of an open-ended question is, "What were the Israelites supposed to do in order to receive the blessings God promised?" Another example of an open-ended question is, "What is a covenant?"

*Closed-ended* questions, on the other hand, are limited in the number of correct or acceptable responses and are generally answered with a "yes" or "no." They are generally easier to answer. Examples of a closed-ended question are "Was John the Baptist a disciple?" or "Was Josiah a successful young ruler?" Try to avoid asking too many yes-or-no questions unless you plan to do further probing.

## FOLLOW-UP QUESTIONS

Another way to use questions is to ask follow-up questions after students have responded to a given question. Examples of follow-up questions include, "How did you arrive at that answer?"; "Will you give an example?"; "Where is that noted in the lesson?"; or, "What Scripture is that found in?"

### Suggestions for Writing Questions
1. Determine your purpose for asking the question. Remember that every question should have a purpose.
2. Prepare questions in advance.
3. Write questions that are relevant and that support the lesson outcomes.
4. Write questions that are clear to students.

## STUDENT-GENERATED QUESTIONS

Give students an opportunity to ask questions. They need to know that their questions are important. When a student asks a question, always acknowledge the person asking the question. Make eye contact with the student when he or she asks the question, and restate (or ask the student to restate) the question before attempting to answer. This not only shows that you are acknowledging the students, but also shows that you are interested in what students are saying and that everyone hears the question.

## QUESTIONING STRATEGIES

Specific questioning strategies can assist students in understanding the lesson more effectively, since they are designed to get students more involved in the lesson. Different questioning strategies that you may want to consider using are listed and described below.

## STOP, THINK, AND WRITE

"Stop, Think, and Write" is a strategy that allows students to think about the lesson as it is read and presented. Students are instructed at the beginning of class to stop and note questions or make notations. This can help them organize their questions (Fister & Kemp, 1996). See page 56.

## THINK-AND-WRITE QUESTIONS

"Think-and-Write Questions" is another questioning strategy that is fun to use. Prior to the presentation of the lesson, have students think of and write questions related to what they want to know about the lesson (Fister & Kemp, 1996).

## SPEAK, LISTEN, AND RESPOND STRATEGY

You may choose to pause from time to time to implement the "Speak, Listen, and Respond Strategy" (Algozzine & Ysseldyke, 1997). This strategy is designed to assess whether students understand the lesson content, and it helps them stay involved with the lesson.

Before you start the lesson, write on the board or post on a chart the following words:
- Summarize
- Questions
- Reactions
- Miscellaneous

Tell the students that after a period of time, you will stop the lesson and ask them to respond to the lesson in one of the formats listed above. You may or may not choose to use all of the words during the lesson. This strategy can be carried out as a whole-group activity, a partner activity, or as a small-group activity. Using this strategy is one way teachers can involve students in the lesson and check their understanding of the lesson at the same time (see page 55).

## WHAT TO DO WHEN YOU DO NOT KNOW

There may be times during your instruction that your students ask questions that you are not able to answer. Do not become alarmed when this happens! This happens to even veteran teachers. When it occurs, do not hesitate to say to your students, "I don't know." Even though we study and prepare, it does not mean that we always have all the answers. Let students know that you will work on getting the answer.

Always do your best to try to have an answer by the next class. You may have to do further research, study, pray, or confer with your pastor, superintendent, or Director of Christian Education to obtain the correct information. You never want to give out wrong and inaccurate information and misguide or mislead your students in any way. Remember, what we say can be a matter of life (eternal) or death (eternal separation) to someone.

# SPEAK, LISTEN, AND RESPOND ACTIVITY

*Directions:*
As we go through our lesson today, we will stop from time to time to do the following:

- **Summarize**
  Summarize important points of the lesson in your own words.

  _____

  _____

  _____

- **Questions**
  Record any questions you might have.

  _____

  _____

  _____

- **Reactions**
  Respond or react to anything you have heard.

  _____

  _____

  _____

- **Miscellaneous**
  Capture your thoughts through writing or some other written format.

  _____

  _____

  _____

Adapted from Algozzine & Ysseldyke (1997).

# Stop, Think, and Write

Lesson: _____ Date: _____

Note: _____
_____
_____
_____

Question: _____
_____
_____
_____

Note: _____
_____
_____
_____

Question: _____
_____
_____
_____

Note: _____
_____
_____
_____

Adapted from Fister & Kemp (1996).

## INQUIRY-BASED LEARNING

We want our students to learn and discover God's truths. One way to do this is through *inquiry-based learning*. Inquiry-based learning is student-centered, involving students actively in the process of learning. It engages students in critical thinking, asking questions, and solving problems. Students are seeking information and answers by asking questions. Thus, asking questions and getting students to think is a big part of this method.

In inquiry-based learning, students gather information about a topic, lesson, or situation by formulating their own questions. After generating their questions, students can work on answering the questions in small groups, in pairs, or individually. Using this method, teachers guide students in finding or discovering the answers themselves. This approach can be used with both youth and adults.

## PROBLEM-BASED LEARNING

In *problem-based learning*, students work collaboratively in a small-group setting to find solutions to real-life problems. The teacher presents students with a problem. This instructional method engages students in analyzing, exploring, researching, and probing, as they discuss ways to solve the problem.

## INDUCTIVE BIBLE STUDY

In this method of instruction, students are engaged in examining the entire Scripture text from general to specific. In other words, a passage is selected for study and is then read. Students begin to observe the text by asking and answering questions to gain further understanding and meaning. You summarize the main point(s) of the passage as you read.

In his article, "Inductive Bible Study Basics," Krejeir (2006) vividly noted that the purpose of the Inductive Bible Study method is to teach how to study the Bible in a logical, clear, and concise way. He further defined *inductive methods* as "a method for learning how to exegete the Bible for all its worth by our best efforts" (p. 1). During this process of Bible study, we observe the text, dig out the meaning, and then apply it to our lives.

Identifying and using specific questions is a part of the inductive Bible study process. For instance, questions are raised to help us study more deeply and learn a selected message of the text. Krejeir gives us the following list as basic inductive Bible study questions to ask. Please note that the first three questions listed are the basic, essential, inductive Bible study questions.

1. What does this passage say?
2. What does this passage mean?
3. What is God telling me?
4. How am I encouraged and strengthened?
5. Is there sin in my life for which confession and repentance are needed?
6. How can I be changed so I can learn and grow?
7. What is in the way of these precepts affecting me? What is in the way of my listening to God?
8. How does this apply to me? What will I do about it?
9. What can I model and teach?
10. What does God want me to share with someone?

## THINK-PAIR-SHARE

"Think-Pair-Share" is a great way to get all students involved in the lesson. It is also a great introductory activity that can be used to prepare students for the lesson. To begin, the teacher poses a question or problem or poses a particular subject, topic, or idea. Students are generally given two to three minutes to reflect on the topic, question, or problem individually (*Think*). Students are then paired with a partner to share their ideas for about five minutes (*Pair*). In the last step, the whole group comes together to share and discuss (*Share*) the most important information about the topic. The pairs share their ideas with the class. This activity gives teachers information on how their students think about a particular topic.

## K-W-L CHARTS

K-W-L is an instructional strategy that helps students identify what they know (K) about a topic, what they want (W) to know, and what they have learned (L). K-W-L charts can be used during the introduction of a lesson to assess students' prior knowledge about a particular topic. The K-W-L chart is generally presented in a three-column format such as the one shown on the following page. In the first column (K), students list "What I Know"; in the second column (W), students list "What I Want to Know." The first two columns are completed by students prior to the lesson. After the presentation of the lesson, students identify in the third column (L), "What I Have Learned." The third column can be used for summarization and assessment. This activity can be completed by students individually, with a partner, in small groups, or with the whole class.

## ANALOGIES

An *analogy* is "a statement in which two things are compared because they have something in common." Jesus used many analogies in His teachings. In analogies, you have two pairs or two sets of words, concepts, or pictures that have similar relationships. Analogies help us see how dissimilar things are similar, and increase our understanding of new information (Campbell & Dickinson, 1996; Marzano, Pickering, & Pollock, 2001).

An example of an analogy is found in the book of John, where Jesus talks about the "Bread of Life." If you were to make an analogy using the "Bread of Life," you would compare physical bread to spiritual bread and its relationship and significance to life. This analogy is a depiction of physical bread as being essential to our physical nourishment, while associating spiritual bread with the Word of God as being essential to our spiritual nourishment.

## REFLECTION ACTIVITIES

In reflection activities, students are asked to reflect and recall something learned from the lesson. To help students think about and reflect on what they have learned, certain questions are asked. Reflection activities not only help students reflect on what they learned, but they also help students retain information. Reflection activities can be completed individually or with a partner, or can be shared as a class activity. Reflection activities can be either verbal or written. Sample reflection activity sheets are displayed on page 60.

# K-W-L

| What Do I Know about Learning Styles? | What Do I Want to Know about Learning Styles? | What Have I Learned about Learning Styles? |
|---|---|---|
|  |  |  |

# Reflection Sheet

**I learned that:**

**I relearned that:**

**I was shown in this lesson that:**

**I can apply what I learn when:**

# 3 - 2 - 1 Activity

**List:**

*Three* **things I learned**

*Two* **things I will share with someone**

*One* **action I will take immediately**

Adapted from The Multiple Intelligences Series (1994).

## VISUAL CHARTS/GRAPHIC ORGANIZERS

Visual charts/graphic organizers are visual instructional tools that can be used in teaching God's Word. They are a great way to organize ideas and information and can be used with all types of learning. These instructional tools can be used at the beginning, during, or at the end of instruction to present information visually, since they are vehicles that help promote student learning and understanding. They can also be used to promote critical thinking.

Visual charts/graphic organizers help students see information and concepts more clearly as they actively engage students in the learning process. These visual charts can be displayed on the blackboard, in flip charts, and in handouts and other formats (diagrams, flow charts, webs, sequence of events, mapping charts, and so forth). They can be completed by the teacher, students individually, with a partner, in small groups, or by the class as a whole.

The following is a description of some of the most commonly employed visual charts or graphic organizers that Christian educators can use in teaching: Cause-Effect, Compare-and-Contrast, Series of Events, Sequential Process, Spider Map, T-charts, the Venn Diagram, and flow charts.

**Cause-Effect:** The *cause* is something that makes something else happen; it is the "why" something happens. An *effect* is what happens as a result of the "cause." Here are some examples of how cause-and-effect scenarios might be set up:
- The effects of _____ were due to _____.
- As a result of _____, then _____ occurred.
- The reason for _____ was due to _____.

To determine the "cause and effect" of a situation, you might ask questions such as these:
- Why do you think that happened?
- How do you think this could have been prevented?

(An example of a cause-and-effect organizer is shown on page 62.)

**Compare-Contrast**: *Compare-Contrast* organizers (see page 63) can be used to show similarities and differences between two things such as people, places, events, ideas, and so forth (Campbell & Campbell, 1996).

**Series of Events:** *Series of Events* organizes events in a specific chronological order or in stages or steps (see page 64).

**Sequential Process:** *Sequential Process* is a description of the stages of events over time. It helps students see the sequence and order of events over time (see page 65).

**Spider Map:** *Spider Maps* are used to describe a central or key idea, a concept, specific persons, events, and things. This graphic design can also be used to list facts, definitions, attributes, or examples related to a single topic, concept, or theme. Examples of spider-map organizers are shown on page 66.

**T-chart:** *T-charts* can be used in many different ways. For example, they can be used to analyze similarities and differences between two things (people, places, events, ideas, and so forth) by placing individual characteristics in either the left or right sections. They can also be used when comparing and contrasting events, people, ideas, and so forth (see pages 67 and 68).

**Venn Diagram:** Two overlapping circles form the Venn Diagram. *Venn diagrams* are commonly used to analyze similarities and differences between two things (people, places, events, ideas, and so forth) by placing separate characteristics in either the left or right sections, and common characteristics within the overlapping section (see page 68).

**Flow Charts:** *Flow Charts* can be simple or complex and can be of any size or shape to display or describe concepts, ideas, and information. They can be drawn on the board, a flip chart, or butcher paper, or cut out and shown as they are explained. You can use different shapes, colors, and sizes in structuring your flow chart. Examples of two types of flow charts are shown on pages 69 and 70.

# Cause-Effect

Topic: _____

| Cause | Effect |
|---|---|
|  |  |
|  |  |
|  |  |
|  |  |
|  |  |
|  |  |
|  |  |
|  |  |
|  |  |

# Compare-Contrast

| Topic | Similarities | Differences |
|---|---|---|
|  |  |  |
|  |  |  |
|  |  |  |
|  |  |  |
|  |  |  |

| Topic | Same | Different |
|---|---|---|
|  |  |  |
|  |  |  |
|  |  |  |
|  |  |  |
|  |  |  |

# Series (or Sequence) of Events

## Topic Examples: Jesus' life work.

1.

2.

3.

4.

5.

## Sequence Organizers

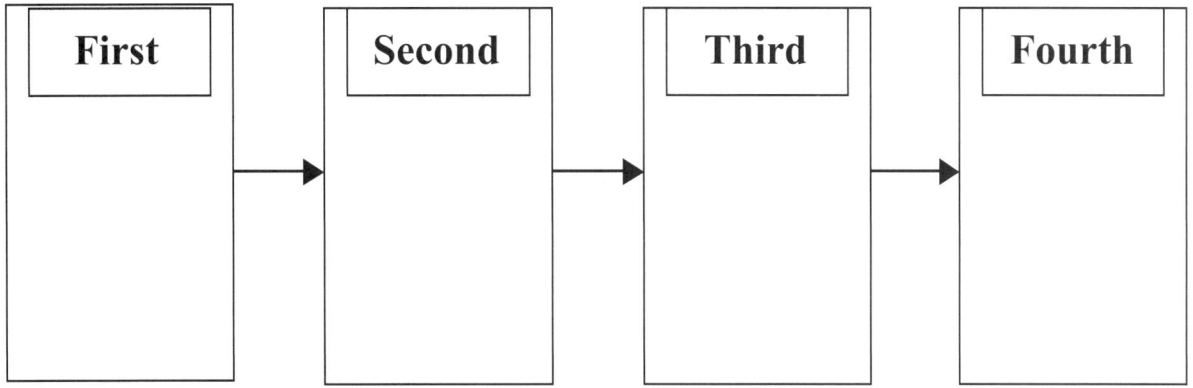

## Sequence of Events

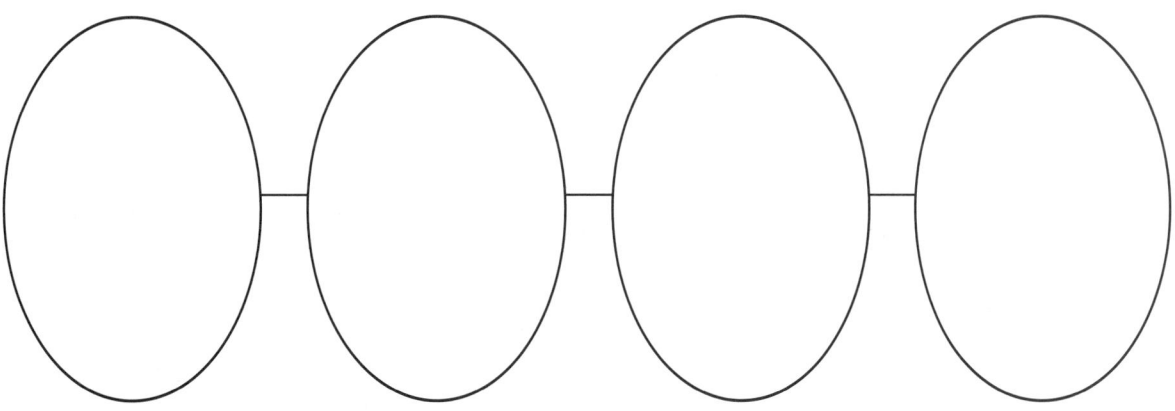

# Spider Map

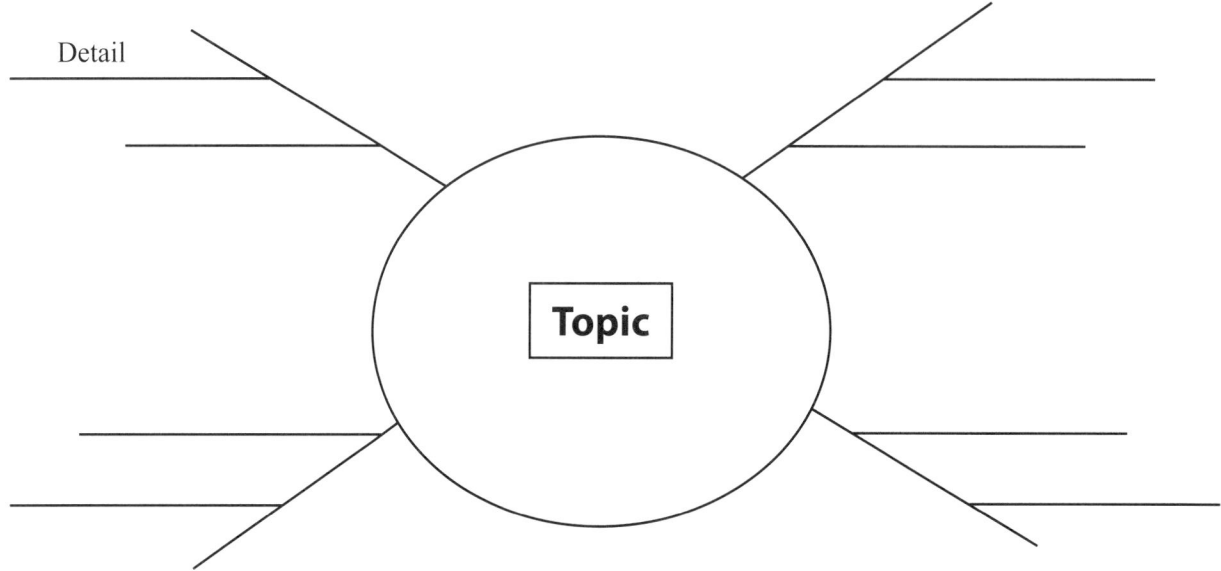

Detail

Topic

Example of a Spider Map based on identifying the characteristics of the prophetess Deborah.

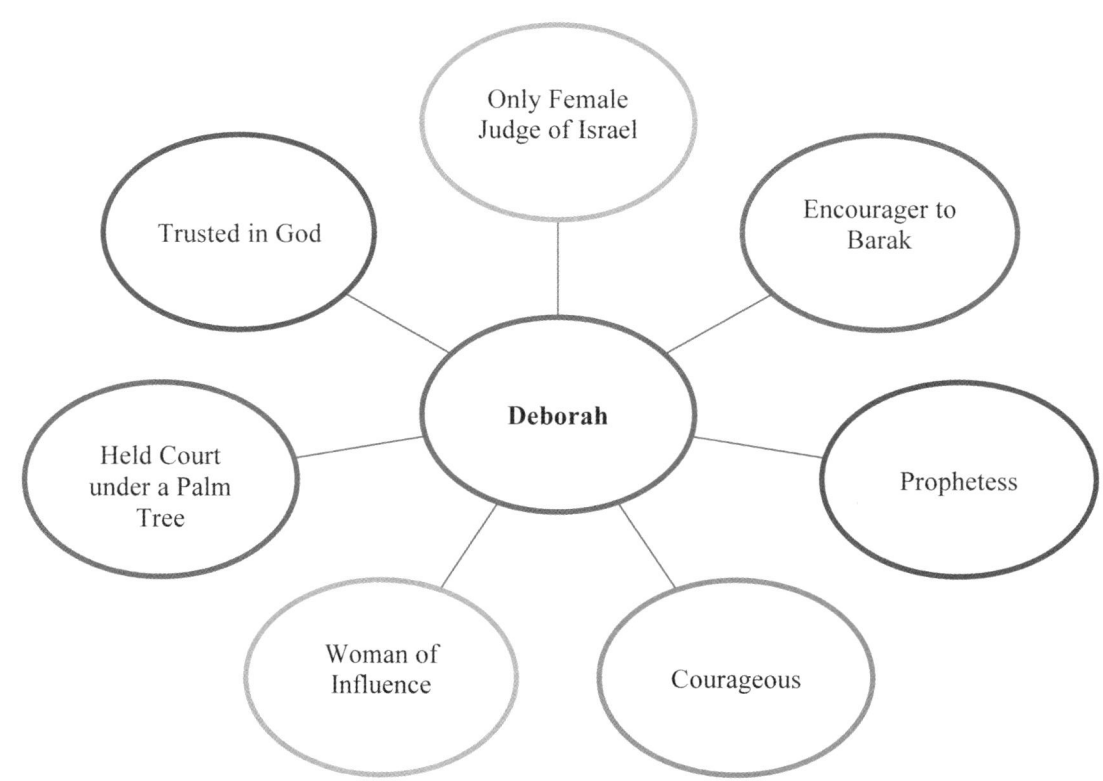

# T-Chart

| Similarities | Differences |
|---|---|
| | |

*Example of a lesson on Zacchaeus using a Compare-and-Contrast T-chart*

| Compare | Contrast |
|---|---|
| **Zacchaeus's life before Christ** | **Zacchaeus's life after Christ** |

*Here is another way to use the T-Chart with students.*

| How I Can Connect Them to My Life | How I Can Connect Them to My Life |
| --- | --- |
|  |  |

## Venn Diagram

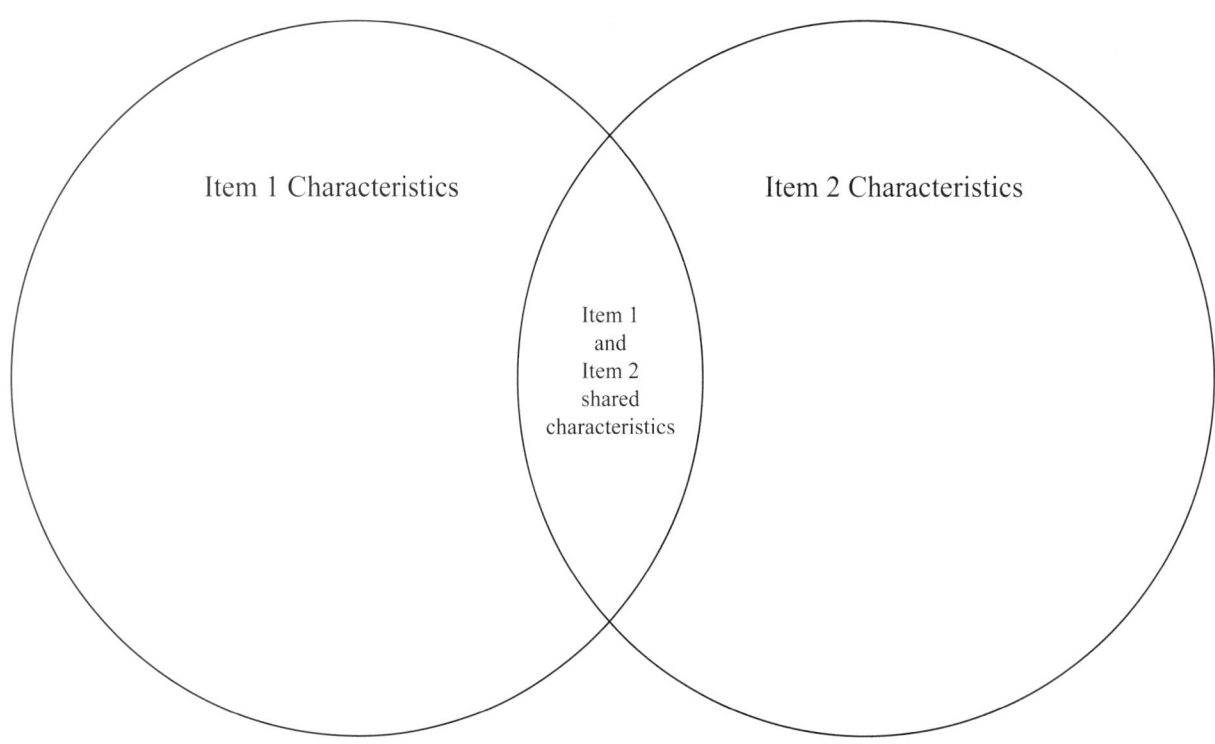

# Sample Flow Chart

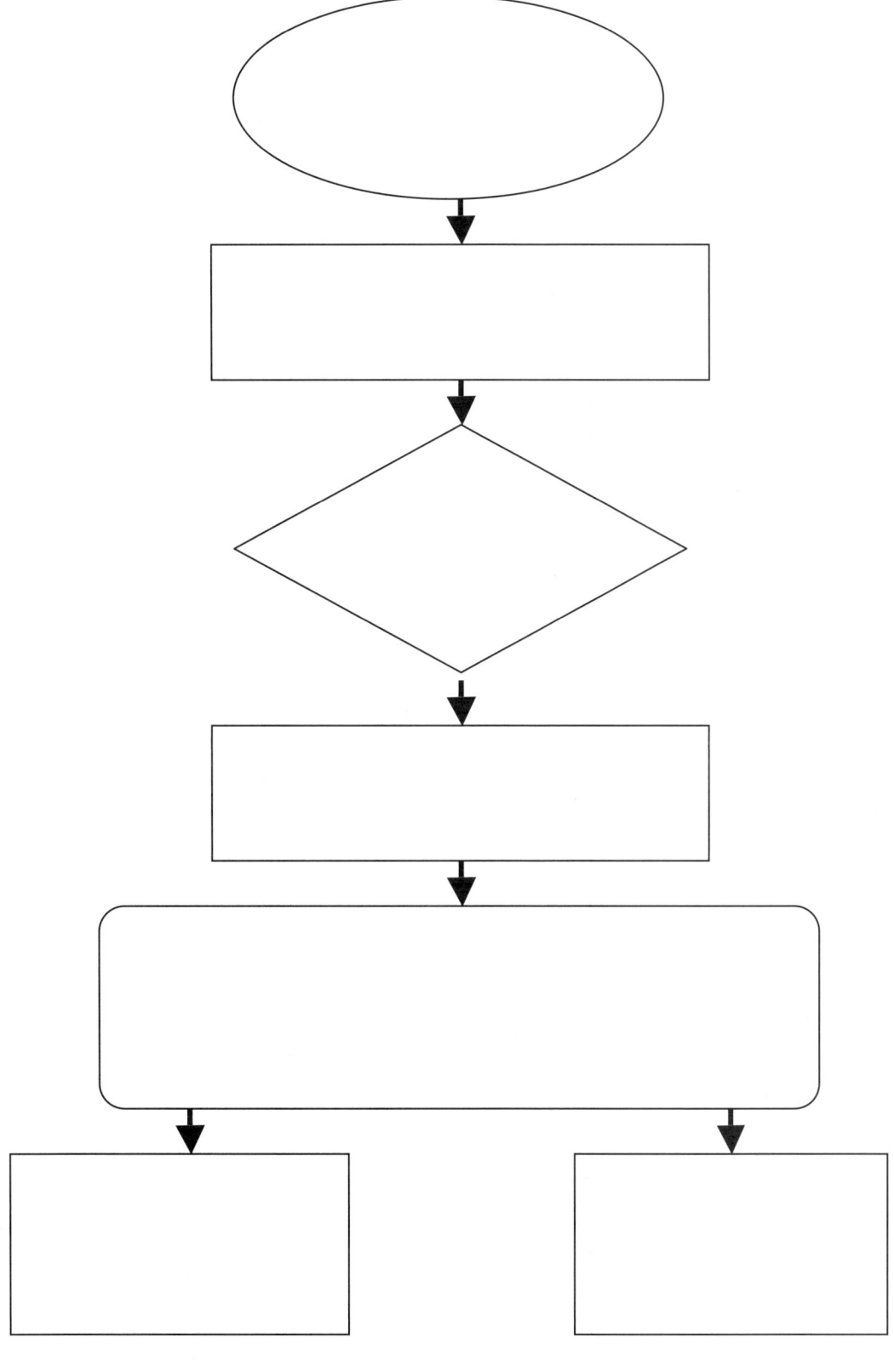

# Sample Flow Chart

Effective Teaching Practices for 21st Century Christian Educators 70

## OUTLINES

Use outlines to list key information and facts that will be presented during the lesson. You can provide students with a format for them to complete as you teach the lesson, or you can have an outline already completed for them to use to follow along with you.

Example of a Lesson Outline:

---

**Lesson Outline**

**Key Words:**


**Key Information:**


**Key Facts:**


**Other Important Points:**

---

## PARTNER AND SMALL-GROUP ACTIVITIES

The use of partners and small groups is an effective way to engage students in the lesson. Some students and adults may hesitate and find it difficult to participate in large-group discussions, but may find it more comfortable discussing and working in small groups. One way to address this concern is to engage students in partner activities, where students work together with another student or partner.

Small groups typically consist of three to five students. Arrange the room so that partners and groups can be seated together. Activities that can be completed with a partner or in small groups include "Think-Pair-Share," brainstorming, reflection, and summarizing. These methods allow students to hear, see, say, do, and redo the activities.

## PARTNER AND SMALL-GROUP SKILLS

Partner and small-group activities cannot work effectively if students lack certain skills. It is a good practice to prepare and equip students with cooperative skills that are needed in order to function effectively in group settings. When students acquire these skills, they will be better-equipped to work more productively in small-group activities. Skills your students need include these:
- Listening
- Sharing
- Taking turns
- Getting along with others
- Handling disagreements
- Respecting others
- Managing conflict and disagreements
- Speaking in quiet and respectful voices
- Giving feedback
- Giving compliments
- Working as a team

## BRAINSTORMING

With this technique, students are asked to list as many ideas as they can on a topic or word in a verbal or written format. The goal of brainstorming is to generate as many ideas, possibilities, or solutions as possible on a given topic in a short period of time. Brainstorming does not judge or evaluate. Brainstorming can be done with the whole class, in small groups, or individually. All responses are recorded. It is important to make sure that everyone is clear on the brainstorming topic. Some examples of a brainstorming question might be these: "When you hear the name *apostle Paul*, what comes to mind?" or "When you think of spiritual blindness, what comes to mind?"

## BUZZ GROUPS

Buzz groups are another way to engage students in discussion. As stated by Campbell and Campbell (1996), in their book, *Teaching and Learning through Multiple Intelligences*, "Teachers can arrange students in groups of three to six to discuss ideas about a particular topic. Each group assigns one person to serve as the recorder, who lists all of the ideas suggested by the group. After several minutes of discussion, the teacher then ask[s] the recorders to summarize the ideas and opinions expressed in his or her group" (p. 16).

## GROUP DISCUSSION

In group discussions, a planned topic, problem, situation, or idea is presented to the group for discussion. A group typically consists of three or more persons. Many dynamics and opinions can arise during classroom discussions, and it can become challenging to keep the discussion on track. As a result, it is imperative that group discussions be planned carefully.
- Leadership, guidelines, rules, and expectations must be established for effective group discussions.
- Someone needs to keep the group focused on the topic, and everyone should have equal access to participate.

- No one person should dominate the discussion. There should be a beginning and ending to the discussion.
- Make sure the main points are summarized and relate them back to the overall aim of the lesson.
- The same skills that are required for small groups to function effectively apply to students engaged in large groups.
- Group discussion is a wonderful way to get opinions and is a way to involve everyone in the discussion.

## CLASS DISCUSSION

Class discussion is a standard way to get the whole class involved. Your role as teacher is to keep the discussion focused on the topic being discussed and to prevent single individuals from dominating the discussion. Give everyone an opportunity to participate. That is why it is important to establish criteria for class discussions. At the end of the class discussion, be sure to allow enough time to summarize the important points discussed.

In her book, *Creative Teaching Methods*, LeFever (1990) lists questions that teachers should ask themselves at the end of the class when students are engaged in discussion activities.

1. In what ways did this discussion contribute to my students' understanding of today's lesson?
2. If each person was not involved, what can I do next week to correct the situation?
3. In what ways did content play a role in the discussion?
4. What followup, if any, should be made on the discussion? (p. 237).

## INTERVIEWS

Interviews can be used in several ways. One way is to form in-group interviews. To begin, divide the class into groups of three and provide the groups with the same question or discussion topic. One person in the group interviews a second person in the group while the third person listens. Then the second person interviews the third person while the first person listens. Finally, the third person interviews the first person while the second person listens. At the end, the teacher brings the whole class together, and each person reports on what he or she heard (LeFever, 1990).

Another way to incorporate the interview method is to generate questions from the lesson. For example, if you are teaching a lesson on forgiveness, you may conduct student interviews by asking students the following question: "Why is it important to forgive?" Students can also be assigned to interview persons outside of their class, asking the same question and reporting the responses to the class.

## PANEL DISCUSSIONS

A panel discussion refers to a small group of students (three or more) who attempt to solve a problem through discussion, with each panelist assigned a specific topic to address. Participants are positioned so they can interact and maintain eye contact with each other. You may select persons to be on the panel who have some specialized interest, knowledge, or expertise on the topic.

To ensure that the panel discussion remains focused on the topic at hand, it is important to give some direction and guidelines to the participants. Organized panels have prepared outlines to follow. The rest of the students should have opportunities to ask questions and interact with the panel.

There are different ways to structure panels. Gangel (1982) outlined three approaches:
1. **The Guided Panel**—The moderator addresses previously prepared questions to the panel.
2. **The Expanding Panel**—In this arrangement, a preliminary and explanatory discussion of a topic is given by a restricted panel. Then the entire group forms a circle to continue the discussion. During this open discussion time, questions may be asked among the group members with panel members serving primarily as resources.
3. **The Reaction Panel**—In this setting, the first thing on the program is a speech, a film, or some other presentation of a point-of-view. Pre-selected panel members then offer a critique of acting with the speaker, or both (p. 51).

## SCRIPTURE SEARCH

Scripture Search is a method in which students are instructed to use their Bibles in class under the guidance and direction of the teacher to search for and locate Scriptures. Scripture searches should be related to the lesson.

## STORYTELLING

Storytelling is another effective way to teach God's Word. Storytelling is regarded as a very vital teaching tool that has been around for thousands of years. Every Christian educator should develop storytelling skills. To be an effective storyteller, you must know the story. If you are telling the story, make sure the content is factual.

As with other methods, storytelling requires preparation and practice. Teachers need to read, re-read, study, and become very familiar with the Bible story they are going to present. Your presentation will be more effective if you know the story. It is important to practice telling the story before telling it to the students. Bible stories should be told or read in an interesting, lively, and dramatic way that captivates your audience by holding their interest and attention.

To be most effective using this method, the storyteller should take on the characters and personalities of those in the Bible story being presented using different voice tones, gestures, expressions, and moods reflected. Be dramatic as you tell the Bible story. Add related visuals and objects to increase interest. For example, if you are telling the story of Noah's Ark, you could have a boat and some animal objects, or you can show pictures of Noah and the ark. You can even use sound effects. By incorporating objects and pictures, you allow your students to visualize the scene and help them get into the meaning and message of the story. It is important to communicate clearly so that all students can understand the story.

Many Bible truths can be taught using storytelling, especially when you engage students in the discussion and ask questions about the story. There are many wonderful stories throughout the Bible, such as the stories of "Cain and Abel"; "Daniel and the lions' den"; "Jonah and the whale"; and "Joseph and his brothers"—all in the Old Testament. In the New Testament, there are stories such as "the good Samaritan"; "the rich young ruler"; "the unjust judge"; and "Zacchaeus the tax collector." Jesus was the Master storyteller, using storytelling as a teaching method on many occasions with His disciples.

## COOPERATIVE LEARNING

In cooperative learning, students work together in small, structured groups or teams on a shared activity. When students are engaged in small-group activities like the ones subsequently mentioned, they are participating in what is known as "Cooperative Learning Groups." Cooperative learning methods promote learning, since students are actively engaged in an interactive process. Remember, as discussed earlier, when students are engaged and involved in their learning, they have a higher retention of what they are learning.

## COOPERATIVE LEARNING ACTIVITIES

The following are some commonly used cooperative learning activities and games that can be incorporated in your teaching. Activities should be clearly explained and modeled with students before being implemented. When selecting a cooperative learning activity, divide the class into small groups or teams and then assign tasks and roles. It is also important that you model the steps to make sure students understand their roles and expectations before they begin.

## ROUND TABLE

Round table is a cooperative learning activity that can be used for brainstorming, reviewing, or practicing. Students sit in teams of three or more around a table. One piece of paper and one pencil is shared by the group. The teacher poses a question or presents a problem that has multiple answers. Students are instructed to brainstorm as many answers as they can to address the question or problem. The sheet of paper is passed around the group clockwise and each student writes an answer. When time is called, the teams with the most correct answers are recognized. Students coach one another when a partner has difficulty. Someone designated from the group will share their responses with the whole group.

## ROUND ROBIN

Here the teacher gives the students a question with multiple answers or a topic problem or concept with multiple parts to discuss. Each student orally provides an answer or contributes to the discussion. Round Robin is the oral counterpart of Round Table.

## NUMBERED HEADS

Using this approach, a team of four is established, and each student is given the numbers 1, 2, 3, and 4. Questions are then asked of each group. Groups work together to answer the questions so that all students can verbally answer them. When the teacher calls out a number, for example "3," then each person who was assigned the number "3" is asked to give the answer. This is a fun way for students to learn and remember material.

## TAKE OFF/TOUCH DOWN

In this activity, all students are seated and the teacher presents a statement or a question. The students stand if they agree and remain seated if they disagree. The correct choice is discussed. This can be a wonderful closing activity to review information presented about the lesson.

## CASE STUDIES

Case studies are "accounts of situations in which a problem is analyzed." This is a good method to use when you are trying to relate a biblical truth to a real-life situation. After reading the case study, students offer suggestions, ideas, and solutions as they analyze the situation. Case studies can be done individually or in small groups. The information is used to reinforce an idea from the lesson.

## ROLE-PLAYING

Role-playing is "an unrehearsed enactment of an event or situation and is less formal than drama." It is a powerful way for students to connect with what is being taught, helping them experience, see, and capture the situation.

Examples of Bible lessons that would lend themselves to role-playing include lessons about "the woman at the well"; "Jesus' washing Peter's feet"; "the good Samaritan"; "Esau and Jacob's reunion"; and "the prodigal son"—just to name a few. Students can also role-play real-life situations related to the lesson, such as situations centered around love, hate, struggles, forgiveness, sharing, and so forth.

To ensure that the role-play goes smoothly, it is important to go over the roles with students ahead of time and give them clear directions. After the role-play is over, have students discuss, analyze, and debrief the message and their experiences. The role-play will not be complete until this happens. This method can be used with both adults and children.

## DRAMA

Drama can also be used to help a class imagine a situation or topic fully. As noted by Campbell and Campbell (1996), through drama participants almost become what they are studying and it is an excellent way to bring the content that you are studying to life. Drama in the classroom can

1. make stories and ideas come alive.
2. pinpoint solutions to problems which people face in real life.
3. stimulate thought on significant issues.
4. reveal insights into the character and personality of persons portrayed in the play.
5. aid the church in evangelism (Gangel, 1982, p. 114).

## SKITS

A *skit* is "a short, usually comic dramatic performance or work." A skit may be written and/or performed by students as a short, humorous interpretation. Students can act out scriptural stories and Bible passages.

## PANTOMIME

*Pantomime* is "a simple form of dramatization in which only actions—no words—are used to communicate a meaning." Students can pantomime Bible stories, Bible characters, and Bible verses. Some songs lend themselves to pantomime as well (Bolton & Smith, 1977).

## MUSIC

There are many different ways to incorporate music into your lessons. Galindo (2006) suggests several different ways you can do this:
- **Play a recording**—Play music as background for small-group work. Highlight a particular song that is related to the lesson.

- *Write a hymn*—Use the tune of a familiar hymn and have the students write new lyrics relating to the topic of the lesson they are studying.

- *Tap out a rhythm*—Have students memorize a passage of Scripture, a key quote, or a proverb and tap out the rhythm of the words. Have students repeat until they have learned the passage by heart.

- *Play musical chairs*—Use musical chairs when studying topics or Bible passages related to being left out, being late, failing to listen, feeling anxious, or being competitive.

According to Bolton and Smith (1977), "A Bible learning activity involving music is an enjoyable way for children to be actively involved in learning and remembering scriptural truths" (p. 178). Music can be used with both children and adults.

## DEBATE

*Debate* is "the exchange of arguments presented orally in a structured format." In debates, students present opposite sides of a controversial issue or topic. One side argues in the affirmative (in support of) and the other side argues the negative (against). They try to persuade others to accept their respective positions. Topics should focus on issues relevant to the lesson.

Each speaker is assigned a time limit for his or her speech. Speakers are also given time to prepare a rebuttal speech. "The burden of proof in a debate is on the affirmative unless the negative side offers an alternative proposal to the one resolved" (Gangel, 1982).

## CREATIVE WRITING

In creative writing, students express their views, opinions, ideas, and creativity on paper. They can write poems and stories which illustrate biblical truths. Creative writing can be used as a supplement to other methods (Gangel, 1982).

## LISTENING TEAMS

Two or more students in a small group or team are instructed to listen to a speaker, a reading, a recording, or something designated by the teacher. After listening, they share their findings with the whole class.

## CONSTRUCTIVE PLAY

Children can begin to learn biblical truths in Sunday school through constructive play activities. Play is important to the development of children. It helps them to develop in all areas—spiritually, cognitively, emotionally, socially, and physically. It is through play that children learn to think, create, and problem solve. As you introduce children to biblical teachings, engage them in play that is stimulating and that will help to develop positive relationships and social skills, such as taking turns, sharing, and being kind. Through constructive play activities, you are laying the foundation for further learning.

## CONCLUSION

As you can see, there are many different types of teaching methods that teachers can use when teaching a lesson. Note that not all methods are applicable to all lessons.

## USE DIFFERENT TEACHING AIDS

Teaching aids can be used for illustration, to make a point, to gain interest and attention, and to assist and support in your instruction. The list of teaching aids is inexhaustible. Some of the common ones are as follows:
- Books
- Chalkboards
- Maps
- Globes
- Atlases
- Flip charts
- Charts
- Butcher paper
- Pictures
- Puppets
- Games
- Flash cards
- Overhead projector slides
- Technology

## TEAM TEACHING OR COLLABORATIVE TEACHING

In team teaching or collaborative teaching, two teachers are assigned to a class and share joint responsibility for planning, teaching, and assessing lesson outcomes. Chase (1977) defined *team teaching* as "The combined efforts of two or more teachers sharing the responsibility for teaching a group of learners" (p. 6). She further stated that team teaching involves teachers planning their lessons together, teaching together, and evaluating together. Teachers share their successes as well as concerns.

In team teaching, teachers build on each other's strengths. They identify and know what their roles are for the class before class time. They also know who will be responsible for certain tasks.

Collaborative teaching is not one teacher teaching one Sunday and the other teacher teaching the next Sunday. Rather, it is two teachers engaged in sharing the teaching responsibility, which may involve their being responsible for different aspects of instruction. Team teaching can take different forms. One form of team teaching is known as "shadow teaching." This is where one teacher presents the lesson while the other teacher is prepared to follow up with additional explanation.

When teachers engage in collaborative teaching in the way that it was designed, the students benefit in many ways. For example, students are exposed to a broader scope of knowledge, learning is enhanced, and students become active learners through frequent interaction and feedback.

Although collaborative teaching has its benefits, team teaching may not be a comfortable arrangement for all teachers. Some teachers simply work better alone.

When using a team-teaching/collaborative-teaching approach, team teachers need to be assigned carefully. Teachers must be compatible in levels of commitment and personality. They need to be able to communicate well with each other, and they need to be able to arrange the time to plan together. Teachers need to feel comfortable in assigning various teaching tasks—who is going to do what. Team teachers must maintain a level of parity in the classroom.

In addition to benefits for students, teachers also benefit from the team approach, as described by Chase (1977). Team teaching

- provides an apprenticeship program for training new teachers.
- provides built-in substitutes.
- allows partners to study the Bible and then discuss it together, which deepens Christian growth and fellowship.
- ensures more adequate preparation.
- makes it easier to recruit teachers, since the responsibility for teaching is shared.

## **POINTS FOR DISCUSSION**

1. Draw a graphic organizer that is appropriate for use when doing a Compare-Contrast. Using the graphic organizer, compare and contrast the differences between traditional methods of teaching versus more effective methods.

2. Identify key factors to consider when selecting an instructional method.

3. Select three to four teaching methods presented in this chapter and describe how you would incorporate them into your teaching.

4. There are a number of factors to consider when making transitions. What are some of them? What are the benefits for your students?

5. You have recently been assigned as a departmental superintendent and you are very interested in implementing a collaborative teaching model with the teachers in your department. Based on the information presented in this chapter, how would you prepare your teachers to teach in a collaborative setting?

# Chapter 7

# Organizing Instruction for Effective Teaching and Learning

How many people will get in their cars and just start driving when they go on a trip? How likely is it that they will arrive at their destination without first knowing where they are going? How will they know when they have arrived? The logical thing to do is to look at a map and chart out the best way to get there. The same principle applies when we plan to teach. Christian educators need to have an organized, systematic plan for teaching each lesson.

## EFFECTIVE TEACHING INVOLVES CAREFUL PLANNING

We discussed earlier the importance of preparation. Part of that time involves the time that you spend in planning and organizing how you are going to teach the lesson. Effective lessons don't just happen. If you expect to teach for results, you must plan for results. Algozzine Ysseldyke and Elliott (1997) state that "planning is a key component of effective teaching" (p. 15). They further stated, "Effective instruction requires planning. This means that effective teachers make decisions before they start teaching. They make decisions about what content to present, about what materials or activities to use and how to present the content and about how to encourage students to approach learning in positive ways" (p. 15).

Effective planning prevents chaos and confusion. Simply put, if you don't plan for it to happen, it may not. Planning how we are going to teach God's Word is very important.

Stronge (2002), in his book, *Qualities of Effective Teachers,* presents a checklist of teacher skills that I believe are most helpful for teachers to consider as they begin to organize and plan for instruction. Some of the indicators he listed are also good checkpoints for Christian educators to follow.

An effective teacher
- carefully links learning objectives and activities.
- organizes content for effective presentation.
- explores student understanding by asking questions.
- considers students' attention spans and learning styles when designing lessons.
- develops objectives, questions, and activities that reflect higher- and lower-level cognitive skills as appropriate for the content and the students (p. 74).

This chapter will help you organize and plan your lesson. As a Christian educator, it is imperative that you plan the best lessons possible because, "If you fail to plan, then you plan to fail." Good teaching begins with good planning.

## LESSON PRESENTATION

Let's begin by looking at the presentation of your lesson. Lessons are typically organized and presented in the format presented on page 81. This page is a description of what generally happens during each phase. Always begin the lesson with some form of worship and then move into the opening phase. Please note that your lesson may not follow the exact order as presented, but most of the components should be included.

**Opening**

- Gain students' attention
- Review
- Create the tone for the lesson
- Introduce the lesson
- Introductory activity
- Present lesson aims and objectives

**Body**

- Bible exploration and explanation
- Teaching procedures
- Lesson instruction

**Closing**

- Summarize/wrap up the lesson
- Review
- Close with activity
- Restate objectives
- Assign homework
- Close with prayer

## SCHEDULING

Some teachers find it helpful to plan their instructional time in a detailed format such as the one shown on page 82. Scheduling helps you organize the different components of your instruction within a specific time frame. In the format shown on the next page, the teacher lists each instructional and class activity and the amount of time allotted for one.

# Class Schedule

**Class:**                                            **Teacher(s):**

**Date:**                                            **Lesson:**

| Lesson Activity | Approximate Time |
|---|---|
|  |  |
|  |  |
|  |  |
|  |  |
|  |  |

## DEVELOPING LESSON PLANS

Carefully developed lesson plans will enhance your teaching skills and help you to become more effective. Having a prepared lesson plan provides a systematic outline and guide to follow when presenting your lesson. Your lesson plan is your detailed plan of instruction—your instructional teaching guide. It helps you to organize the lesson and present it in an orderly way. More specifically, lesson plans are written descriptive outlines of what you are going to do and how you are going to do it. Think of your lesson plan as your written guide for instruction. It provides focus and direction on what you are trying to accomplish.

By the time you are ready to develop your lesson plan, you should have a clear idea of what you are going to teach and how you are going to teach it. Then you need to have an organized, systematic way of presenting the lesson. The Bible says that we should do things "decently and in order." That includes how we teach God's Word.

It takes time to develop effective lesson plans. Lesson plans should be well-thought-out and purposeful, with the lesson aim in mind. Everything in your lesson plan should be interrelated in some way. In other words, every activity and outcome should connect to the aim of the lesson. Allow yourself plenty of time to develop your lesson plan. Remember to begin early. In fact, you should begin formulating ideas for your lesson plan during your study and preparation phase.

A variety of lesson plan guides and formats may be used when planning a lesson. One such format is presented and described in this chapter. A simple format is also presented at the end of the chapter. Whether they develop their own or not, all Christian educators should have an understanding of the lesson plan process and how it can enhance their ability to teach more effectively.

The intent of the remaining chapter is to help you to learn to write effective lesson plans. Following and completing each of the nine steps is important. Remember, effective planning plus prayer and preparation results in effective teaching.

Step 1    Lesson Objectives
Step 2    Materials/Resources/Supplies
Step 3    Lesson Introduction/Opening
Step 4    Methods/Procedures and Activities
Step 5    Lesson Conclusion/Closure
Step 6    Assignments
Step 7    Follow-up
Step 8    Evaluation and Reflection of the Lesson

## STEPS TO EFFECTIVE LESSON PLANNING

## STEP 1: WRITE LESSON OBJECTIVES/OUTCOME(S)

The first step in developing a lesson plan is to identify and write the lesson outcome(s) or objectives for the lesson you are preparing to teach. I use the words *outcomes* and *objectives* interchangeably, with both of them referring to the same idea.

Your lesson objectives should be identified before you begin teaching. "When we identify our objectives before we begin teaching, we are in a better position to choose an effective method of instruction" (Ormond, 2000, p. 519). Lesson outcomes are important to teaching. They are the foundation on which to build your lesson. They guide your instruction, teaching materials, and content. Objectives specify what you want your students to learn, know, and/or do. They are specific, observable, and measurable.

As you begin to write your objectives, ask yourself two important questions: What do I expect or want to happen in the lives of my students from the teaching of this lesson? What do I want my students to learn and experience from the lesson?

The outcome(s) or objectives determine to a degree what you will teach and how you will teach it. Rushbuldt (1981) writes, "The best way to write objectives is to include in them the types of outcomes you expect from your teaching" (p. 57). Additionally, Rule and Lord (2003) note, "For any given curriculum, knowing the intended outcome or objective determines the **what**, **how**, and **when** of teaching" (p. 4).

*Learning outcomes* are clear statements written that address what a teacher wants students to learn, experience, demonstrate, do, discover, and receive as a result of the lesson. In other words, they should answer this question: "What do you want your students to know and be able to do at the end of the lesson?" As you begin to identify your objectives, you may find it helpful to generate a list of outcomes for the lesson you are preparing to teach and then narrow the list to two to three key outcomes.

## TYPES OF OBJECTIVES

There are three common types of objectives: Cognitive, Affective, and Psychomotor.

**Cognitive**—The cognitive domain involves knowledge and the development of intellectual skills and abilities. It is in this domain that students recall or engage in the recognition of specific facts, information, and concepts.

**Affective**—The affective domain addresses our emotions and feelings and the manner in which we deal with things emotionally. It involves our feelings, values, and attitudes about what we have learned.

**Psychomotor**—This is what the student will demonstrate physically as evidenced by the use of fine or gross-motor skills. The psychomotor domain involves some form of physical movement, involvement, or activity that is a focus on physical and kinesthetic skills. It is a good practice to consider writing objectives that reflect the three domains listed above.

## CONSIDERATIONS WHEN WRITING LEARNING OUTCOMES/OBJECTIVES

Effective Christian educators write their instructional objectives carefully. There are some key variables to consider when writing learning or instructional outcomes/objectives.

1. Make sure the outcomes are clear and specific and are presented at the beginning of the lesson.
2. Direct the outcomes toward what you are teaching and what students are learning.
3. Structure your lesson and methods of presentation in such a way that the objectives can be met.
4. Plan your lesson in such a way that student outcomes can be achieved.
5. Think about ways students can achieve these outcomes.
6. Determine how you will assess whether students met the outcomes.

Additionally, there are two key questions that should be addressed:
- What do I want my students to learn from this lesson?
- How am I going to evaluate and determine if students accomplished the objective(s) for the lesson?

When writing your objectives, keep them brief, simple, specific, clear, and to the point. Additionally, good outcomes have a time frame, are written using action verbs, and identify what the student will be able to do (Rushbuldt, 1981). Avoid using unnecessary words. Identify in the objective exactly what you want your students to be able to know and do as a result of the lesson. Write your objectives in positive terms, such as "Students will explain…"; "By the end of the lesson, students will be able to describe…"; or, "From this lesson, students will be able to differentiate between…." Having lesson objectives will let students know what they will be expected to learn.

At the end of the lesson, you should have some evidence that students achieved the listed outcomes. Lesson outcomes will let you know how well students learned and understood the lesson presented.

A way to help you write good instructional outcomes/objectives is to use *Bloom's Taxonomy of Educational Objectives*, as previously discussed in chapter 6.

*Bloom's Taxonomy* is a classification system that helps the teacher write objectives in clear terms. It can serve as a guide and reference tool to use when writing student outcomes for your lesson.

There are six categories or levels: Knowledge, Comprehension, Application, Analysis, Synthesis, and Evaluation. They are listed in order on the following page, starting from the simplest behavior (knowledge) to the most complex (evaluation), along with a definition for each category, verbs, and sample objectives (Bull & Land, 1985; Huitt, 2004; Rule & Lord, 2003).

# Bloom's Taxonomy

| Category | Definition | Sample Action Verbs to use in writing objectives | Sample Question Starters |
|---|---|---|---|
| **Knowledge** | Recalling and reciting information learned | Write<br>Name/Recite<br>Identify<br>Recall<br>State<br>Define/Explain | What did Paul say about…?<br>List three…<br>How would you explain…?<br>Can you name…? |
| **Comprehension** | Basic level of understanding; the ability to grasp the meaning | Explain<br>Discuss<br>Summarize<br>Describe<br>Paraphrase<br>Compare/Contrast | How would you summarize…?<br>Describe what happened when…<br>Can you put it in your own words? |
| **Application** | Applying information/ knowledge to a new situation | Demonstrate<br>Show<br>Produce<br>Complete<br>Discover<br>Prepare<br>Share | What examples can you find in the lesson that supports…?<br>How would you apply what happened to…? |
| **Analysis** | Breaking down into parts | Categorize<br>Compare<br>Analyze<br>Examine<br>Classify<br>Discuss<br>Probe | What conclusions can you draw from this lesson?<br>If…had happened, then what might the end results have been? |
| **Synthesis** | Creating, making, doing something; stresses creative behaviors | Compose<br>Construct<br>Develop<br>Prepare<br>Compile<br>Create<br>Generalize | What would have happened if…?<br>Do you believe… and why?<br>What is a possible solution to…? |
| **Evaluation** | Making a judgment about something; contains elements of all of the other categories | Assess/Evaluate<br>Compare<br>Interpret<br>Judge<br>Recommend<br>Justify<br>Critique | How would you compare the people's actions then to today?<br>What do you think about? |

## BLOOM'S REVISED TAXONOMY

A former student of Benjamin Bloom, along with a group of others, revised the taxonomy. The purpose was to add relevance for students and teachers in the twenty-first century (Forehand, 2005). The six major categories were changed from nouns to verbs. Subcategories of the six major categories were also replaced by verbs. The "old" and the "new" taxonomies are shown at the bottom of this page along with word changes that describe the different levels (Pohl, 2000). Note that the original "Evaluation" term goes with the new term "Evaluating" and the term "Synthesis" goes with the new term "Creating."

### Bloom's Taxonomy

| Revised Version | Original Version |
|---|---|
| **Creating**<br>*Can the student create new products or points of view?* | Synthesis |
| **Evaluation**<br>*Can the student justify a decision or course of action?* | Evaluation |
| **Analyzing**<br>*Can the student distinguish between the different parts?* | Analysis |
| **Applying**<br>*Can the student use the information in a new way or in another familiar situation?* | Application |
| **Understanding**<br>*Can the student explain ideas or concepts?* | Comprehension |
| **Remembering**<br>*Can the student recall or remember the information?* | Knowledge |

## STEP 2: MATERIALS/RESOURCES/SUPPLIES

The function of this step is to help teachers determine and organize in advance the materials and resources they need to present their lesson. Ask, identify, list, and determine the following:
1. What materials are needed to teach the lesson?
2. What materials do I need to prepare and/or assemble in advance?
3. What materials do my students need?
4. What materials do I already have that I can use?
5. How much time will it require to prepare the materials?
6. What equipment do I need (PowerPoint, overhead projector, flip chart, and so forth)?
7. Do I need to practice using the equipment before I use it?
8. Do I need assistance to use the equipment?
9. What materials do I need to purchase or request for purchase?
10. What additional books or resources are needed?

After determining the materials/resources/supplies needed, make a list, and begin gathering what you need to teach your lesson. Be creative! Some things you can make yourself, while others you can borrow. There may be a need to purchase, or you may already have items on hand. Regardless of how you gather your materials, it is important to the success of your lesson that you have everything ready before your class starts. Identifying materials needed for the class ahead of time is a part of the planning process. Things tend to run smoother with less stress when you take the necessary time to plan and prepare ahead. On the following page is a checklist that can assist you in planning for your materials, resources, and supplies.

# Materials/Resources/Supplies Checklist

Lesson _____     Date _____

| | Items I already have | Items to borrow | Items to buy | Items to make and prepare |
|---|---|---|---|---|
| Materials needed to teach the lesson: | | | | |
| Equipment needed: | | | | |
| Materials and supplies for students: | | | | |
| Books/resources: | | | | |

## STEP 3: LESSON INTRODUCTION/OPENING

Your lesson introduction/opening is a very important step of your lesson and should be planned carefully. Lessons should begin on time with excitement and enthusiasm. It is during the introduction that you "hook" your students and gain their interest and attention. You are getting them ready for the lesson as you are setting the tone for the lesson. Most importantly, you are getting your students ready to learn and discover important biblical truths. As stated by Rushbuldt (1981), "How you open your session usually determines what will happen during the session" (p. 59).

There are many different ways you can introduce your lesson. For example, you can:
1. review and state the lesson aim and outcomes/objectives for the lesson.
2. review student expectations.
3. give a general overview on what you are going to teach and do.
4. review last week's lesson.
5. relate this lesson to a previous lesson.
6. go over key words/terms/names in the lesson.
7. provide background information and other information that students need to know prior to the presentation of the lesson.
8. provide a brief overview of the lesson.
9. give students specific instructions for the lesson.
10. identify and define key words in the lesson.
11. review assignment/homework.
12. do a short activity to get the students ready for the lesson.
13. ask a thought-provoking question as a lead-in to the lesson.

Everything you do in the introduction phase should prepare and get your students ready for the lesson. As mentioned, as you begin, it is critical that you not only gain the attention of your students, but keep their attention throughout the lesson as well. The introduction phase can also be a time when you assess your students' prior knowledge of the lesson. Prior knowledge is what students already know about a particular topic.

As noted earlier in chapter 2, your students will come to your class with different levels of experiences, different levels of background knowledge, and different abilities. In assessing a student's prior knowledge, it may be helpful to determine in advance how to assess what students already know and what the students need to know prior to teaching the lesson. Also, you may want to think about how you are going to link what students already know about the lesson to what you will be teaching. You want to make sure that you continue to build on what students already know.

## INTRODUCTION ACTIVITIES

As described in the table on page 90, there are many ways to introduce a lesson. Prayerfully and carefully select the most appropriate introductory activities for your class. Keep in mind as you plan your introduction that all activities should be meaningful and purposeful and relate in some way back to the lesson. Additionally, determine how much time you are going to allow for your opening activities. You do not want to spend more time on the introduction and opening than you do on your lesson. If you have a sixty-minute teaching period, the following is an example of what that time might look like.

| | | | | |
|---|---|---|---|---|
| Introduction | 5-7 minutes | | | |
| Lesson | 30 minutes | | | |
| Activities | 15-20 minutes | | | |
| Closing | 5-7 minutes | | | |

Below are some suggested activities that can be used during the introduction phase of the lesson.

## Introduction Methods and Activities

| | | | | |
|---|---|---|---|---|
| K-W-L | Questions | Group activities | Games | Group discussions |
| Pre-quiz (oral or written) | Brainstorming | Compare-Contrast | Think-Pair-Share | Demonstrations |
| Oral presentations | Scenarios | Worksheets | Pictures/ diagrams | Partner activities |
| Videos | Analogies | Review of a current event related to the lesson | Simulations | Role-plays |
| Creative writing/ drawings | Illustrations | Reflection activities | Storytelling | Graphic organizer |

## STEP 4: TEACHING METHODS/PROCEDURES

In this step, you determine and list the teaching methods and activities you plan to use in teaching the lesson (lecture, group discussion, questions and answers, storytelling, role-play, and so forth). Again, teaching methods are merely the different ways used to teach a lesson. As you select a method(s) for teaching, keep in mind that all teaching methods and activities selected should be relevant and appropriate for the lesson and that not every method is appropriate for every lesson. Teaching methods should be carefully and prayerfully selected and designed in such a way that they help students meet the objectives listed for the lesson.

When selecting teaching methods and activities, the following factors should be considered:
- The size of the group
- Students' age group
- Relationship and application of the method to the lesson
- Students' level of understanding
- Size of the room
- Amount of teaching time allotted
- The different ways people learn
- The lesson itself (some methods are more appropriate for certain lessons than others)
- The appropriateness and meaningfulness of the method

Additional questions to consider:
1. Does the method/activity help reinforce and teach the biblical truths of the lesson?
2. Does the method/activity allow for all students to participate?
3. Does the method/activity contribute to students' applying the biblical truths to everyday life?

It is important to involve and engage your students in the lesson. Students learn better when they are actively involved and engaged in the learning process. Learn to use a variety of methods. In other words, do not get stuck in the rut of using the same methods all of the time. As stated by Gangel (1982), "The teacher who wishes to be really effective will be sure that his teaching is characterized by variety" (p. 10).

## TEACHING AND ASSESSMENT

We must seek to know throughout the lesson that our students are connecting with the lesson. To do so, we must engage in some form of assessment, check, or feedback from our students. Determine in advance how you will determine, identify, and check for student understanding and attainment of the lesson content. Just as you plan how you are going to teach the lesson, you also need to plan how you are going to assess your students' understanding of the lesson. Teaching and assessing are essential parts of the teaching-learning process.

Effective teachers don't wait until the end of the lesson to assess for understanding. Rather, they are engaged in the process of checking and assessing student knowledge and understanding throughout the lesson. You do not want your students to leave your class confused, baffled, and unclear about the Bible truths you are teaching.

One way to check for student understanding is to ask questions. Answers signal whether your students understand the lesson and also let you know what they are thinking. Based on students' answers, you can go back and adjust your instruction and methods to ensure that you are reaching all of your students.

Assessment is
- ongoing.
- reviewing.
- a reflection of understanding.
- tied to lesson outcomes.
- used to measure the effectiveness of the lesson.
- used to improve instruction.

***The teaching and assessment cycle should look like this:***

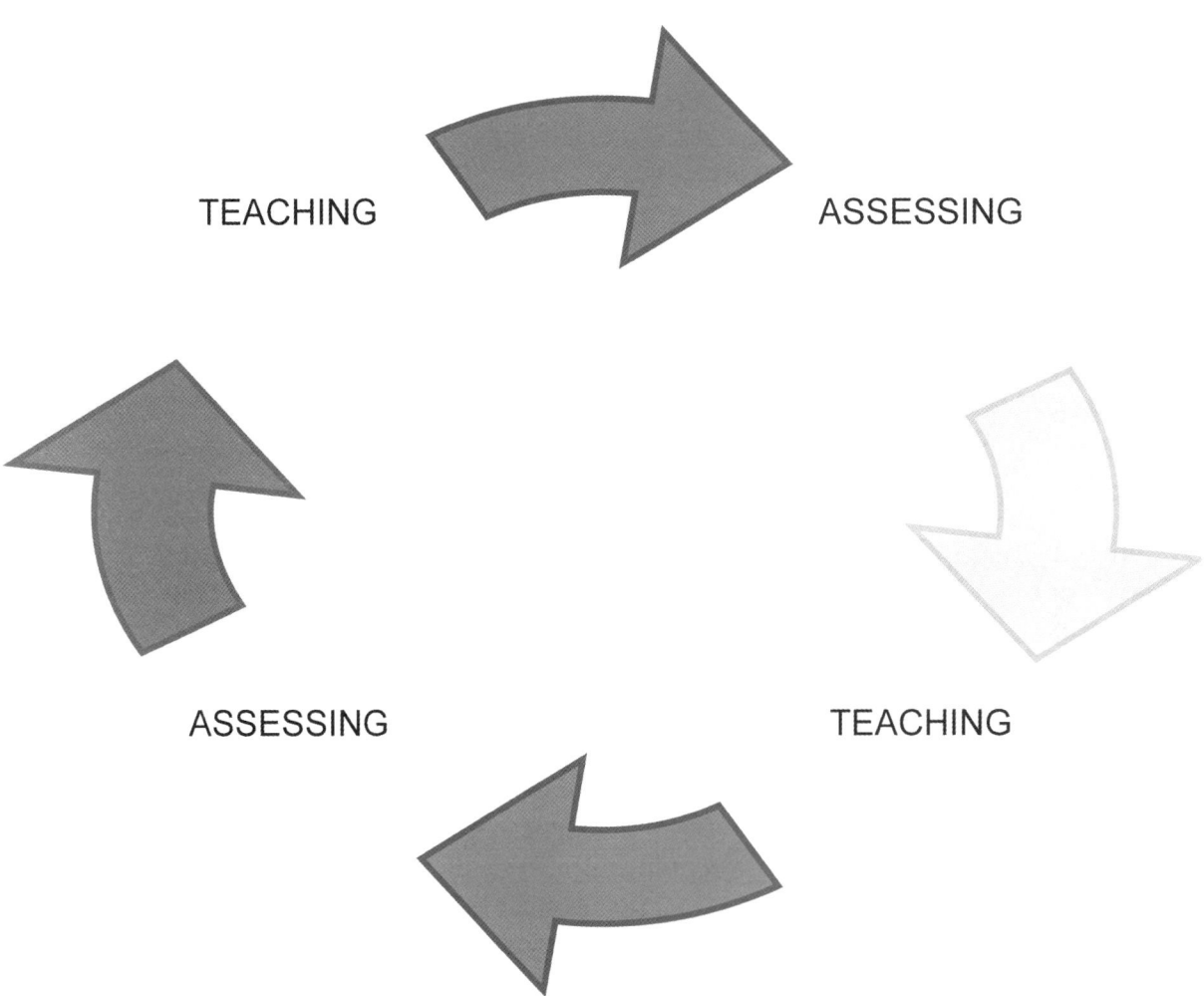

On the following page is an example of a fun sample lesson review activity that can be used to assess student knowledge after the completion of a lesson. This format is easy to develop.

# SAMPLE LESSON REVIEW

*This review of the lesson can be done individually, with a partner, in small groups, or as a class activity.*

*This sample lesson review is based on a lesson about Amos.*

| True or False (Circle One) | Fill in the Blank | Multiple Choice |
|---|---|---|
| **True or False?** The Israelites admired judges who reproved evildoers and witnesses who spoke the truth. | Amos made a plea for the wicked to _____. | Amos was: <br> a. a major prophet. <br> b. a Levite. <br> c. a minor prophet. |
| **True or False?** God still watches the treatment of the poor and downtrodden today. | The prophet Amos urged the Israelites to seek _____ rather than _____ so they could live. | God was calling for the Northern Kingdom to: <br> a. keep doing what they were doing. <br> b. repent. <br> c. appoint more judges. |
| **True or False?** Righteousness indicates that people are in right relationship with God. | Amos prophesied to the _____ Kingdom in Israel. | God told the people through Amos that if they would turn away from evil, they would have: <br> a. more land. <br> b. more prosperity. <br> c. His mercies. |
| **True or False?** Amos was one of the major prophets. | Amos' message was _____ in Israel. | What words did God use to denounce Israel's worship? <br> a. I despise… <br> b. I love… <br> c. I disprove… |
| **True or False?** The dual emphasis on *justice* and *righteousness* runs throughout the book of Amos. | God should be the _____ of our worship. | Amos saw Israel's fate as: <br> a. hopeless. <br> b. positive. <br> c. peaceful. |

## STEP 5: LESSON CONCLUSION/CLOSURE

This is where you decide how you are going to wrap up the lesson. Make sure to plan and allow ample time for your conclusion. Never leave your students dangling and wondering as the lesson comes to an end. The conclusion can be a very powerful component of your lesson. It is during this time that your students could be making serious decisions about what has been said and what it means to their lives.

Below are listed some ways to conclude your lesson. As with the other parts of the lesson, it is a good practice to involve your students in some way in the conclusion of the lesson. The following are different components that can be a part of your conclusion:

1. Summary/recapitulation and/or review of main points addressed in the lesson (students or teacher);
2. Overview of the unit of lessons;
3. Closing activity;
4. Student reflection activities;
5. Students showing or telling what they learned;
6. Drawing conclusions from the lesson (students or teacher);
7. Prayer;
8. Invitation to discipleship; and,
9. Preview of next week's lesson.

## STEP 6: ASSIGNMENTS FOR NEXT WEEK

You may want to give your students assignments or special projects to work on for next week's lesson. If so, this is the step where you determine what those assignments might be. Additional preparations needed by the students for the following lesson should also be determined before the end of class. Make sure students understand specifically what the assignment is and what your expectations are.

## STEP 7: FOLLOW-UP

Your duties as a Christian educator extend beyond the mere forty-five minutes or one hour of teaching time on Sunday mornings. Effective Christian educators do some form of follow-up with their students during the week. Their concern for their students is manifested in some way. At the end of each lesson, stop and take time to ask yourself the following: "What students do I need to call, visit, or just follow up with for next Sunday?" Then, schedule time during the week so you can do the necessary follow-up with your students.

## STEP 8: ASSESSMENT/EVALUATION

In this step, you determine how you are going to assess your teaching and how you are going to critique the progress of the lesson. Step 8 is a very important part of the lesson plan and teaching process. Assessing and evaluating your teaching is essential to gathering information about the effectiveness of your teaching. To be effective in your teaching you must monitor, evaluate, and revise and adjust your instructional methods to reach all students. In order to get the best results, this should be done immediately following the lesson.

There are different ways to assess a lesson. One way to assess your effectiveness is to use some form of self-assessment. *Self-assessment* is your own personal reflection on how well the lesson went. Information gathered from the self-assessment can be used when preparing future lessons, as it also helps in identifying your strengths and weaknesses. To get an accurate picture of your teaching, you must be honest, open, and objective when evaluating lessons.

Rushbuldt (1981) suggested some basic questions that you can ask to organize your thinking about what happened as a result of the lesson you taught. Some of the questions he suggests for you to consider are:
1. How well did you organize to teach the lesson?
2. Did you make all the necessary arrangements for materials and resources?
3. How well did things go?
4. Do you feel that the whole teaching experience went smoothly?
5. Did the opening activities flow smoothly into the next step?
6. Did the selected teaching activities blend well with other steps, the classroom setting, the number of persons present, and so forth? Did anything happen to or for the students?
7. Did the learning objectives produce results?
8. Were the students equipped to do what you wanted them to be able to do by the end of the session?
9. What happened that makes you think you accomplished your objective(s)? (p. 64)

As you reflect on how the lesson went, here are some additional questions that you might want to consider:
1. Did I carry out my lesson plan effectively?
2. Did I teach the lesson using different modalities?
3. Were my methods effective?
4. Were the learning outcomes achieved?
5. Did I reach all of my students?
6. Am I pleased with the way the lesson went?
7. What went well?
8. What didn't go so well or got out of hand?
9. What would I do differently next time?
10. What did I enjoy most about teaching this lesson?

Feedback from your students is another way to gather information about the assessment of a lesson. There are different ways you can obtain feedback information from your students, such as
- questionnaires
- interviews
- checklists
- feedback sheets
- reflection sheets
- comment boards
- discussion at the end of the lesson

Also, just by observing your students' behaviors in class and their actions and reactions to what is being said offers important clues. Additionally, their level of interest and their response to certain situations can provide you with important feedback clues. Sample assessment and evaluation forms are shown on pages 96-98.

## SAMPLE TEACHER SELF-ASSESSMENT

1. My teaching methods were effective.
   **List an example:**
   _____
   _____
   _____

2. I was able to connect with and reach all of the students in my class.
   **List an example:**
   _____
   _____
   _____

3. Every student had an opportunity to participate in the lesson.
   **List an example:**
   _____
   _____
   _____

4. The lesson went the way I anticipated.
   **List an example:**
   _____
   _____
   _____

5. The lesson did not go the way I anticipated.
   **List an example:**
   _____
   _____
   _____

   **Notes:**
   _____
   _____
   _____
   _____
   _____
   _____
   _____
   _____

# Sample Lesson Evaluation Checklist

|  | Response | | |
|---|---|---|---|
|  | Yes | No | Comment |
| 1. I came to my class prepared with a lesson plan. | | | |
| 2. I taught the lesson using different modalities of learning. | | | |
| 3. My teaching methods and activities were effective for the lesson presented. | | | |
| 4. I am pleased with the outcome of the lesson. | | | |
| 5. Students were given opportunities to participate in the lesson. | | | |
| 6. I am pleased with the amount of participation that occurred. | | | |
| 7. Outcomes were met. | | | |
| 8. Students received what I wanted them to receive from the lesson. | | | |
| 9. I will do some things differently next time (if yes, list below). | | | |
| 10. I was able to connect with each of my students. | | | |

Additional Comments:

_____

_____

_____

_____

_____

_____

_____

_____

_____

# Lesson Assessment

**Lesson** _____ **Date** _____

| What went well? | What did not go well? |
| --- | --- |
|  |  |

The lesson assessment format (T-chart) shown on this page may be used to assess your teaching on a weekly, monthly, quarterly, or yearly basis. Conduct an analysis of both columns. Identify variables applicable to each column. Look at what you want to change and improve. Make a plan.

# Lesson Plan

| Date: | Lesson: | Scripture: |
|---|---|---|

Lesson Objectives:

Instructional Materials/Resources/Supplies Needed to Teach This Lesson:

Lesson Introduction:

Teaching Methods/Procedures:

Activities:

# Lesson Plan

Main Points to Address:

Lesson Conclusion/Closure:

Assignments:

Follow-up:

Assessment/Evaluation:

# Sample Lesson Plan

| Date 11.18.07 | Lesson God Preserved a Remnant | Scripture Genesis 45:1-12 |
|---|---|---|

## Lesson Objectives
- Students will describe Joseph's emotional encounter with his brothers.
- Students will discuss Joseph's provisions for his family.
- Students will generalize Joseph's situation in lieu of what God did then, to what He can do in the lives of His people today.

## Lesson Introduction
- Ask for a volunteer to give a brief review of last week's lesson.
- Use a summary of the previous lesson as a lead-in to today's lesson.
- Ask "What is reconciliation?" Define the term.
- Ask students to think about a time when they engaged in reconciliation with someone and what that was like—have them think about it. If time allows, have one to two persons briefly share their experiences and responses.

## Methods/Procedures
- Role-play the Scripture lesson text.
- Hold group discussion.
- Ask questions. "What was the reaction of Joseph's brothers when he disclosed his identity to them? Describe Joseph's reaction to his brothers. How would you have reacted if you were in Joseph's shoes? How was God's providential hand at work in the life of Joseph?"

## Activities
Small-group activity: Read and discuss Romans 8:28 and its implications for this lesson.

## Instructional Materials/Resources Needed to Teach This Lesson
- Bible
- Pencils
- Overhead projector-list questions
- Overhead projector pens
- Reflection sheets

# Sample Lesson Plan

## Main Points to Address
- God had a plan and a purpose to save Joseph and his family.
- Joseph's situation was in God's plan.
- Joseph made provisions for his family.
- What may be a bad, difficult situation may be for our good.
- God has a plan and design for your life.
- Forgiveness and repentance.
- God had ordained Joseph's footsteps.
- God can take a bad situation and turn it around for good and His glory.
- God made a promise to Abraham and his descendants that they would multiply.

## Conclusion
- Complete a reflection sheet and share and discuss with a partner.
- Summarize main points addressed.
- Close with a prayer on forgiveness.

## Follow-up
- Will be determined at the end of class.

## Assignments
- Assign students to read Genesis 48:8-21 for next week's lesson.

## Evaluation
- Complete a self-evaluation checklist.

# Lesson Plan

Date: _____

Lesson: _____  Scripture: _____

Objectives: _____
_____
_____
_____

Materials: _____
_____
_____
_____

Introduction/Entry: _____
_____
_____
_____

Instructional Procedures: _____
_____
_____
_____

Activities: _____
_____
_____
_____

Closure: _____
_____
_____
_____

## **POINTS FOR DISCUSSION**

1. Describe and discuss the basic steps involved in developing a lesson plan.

2. Think back to a lesson you taught recently and complete the sample teacher evaluation form. What did you learn from your responses?

# Chapter 8

# Teaching and Technology

We live in a technology-driven culture often aptly referred to as the "Information Age." Technology has changed the way we communicate with each other and has opened the door to a wealth of information and resources. Today's generation of young people has grown up with technology. For many, technology is integrated into their everyday lifestyles. As a result, many of your students are using technology on a daily basis, including video games, DVDs, CDs, computers, the Internet, cell phones, and other technological devices.

Technology has become a significant part of educational systems today and will remain so in the future. Given that we live in a technological world, Christian educators should develop an understanding of different technologies that can assist them in becoming even better-equipped and more effective teachers.

To be relevant and up-to-date, Christian educators must be open to learning about and adapting to the use of technology as a part of their lesson preparation and use. This includes using technology as a way to enhance instruction, present lessons, gather resources, and engage students.

Technology can be used in your classroom to enhance your instruction and help you become even more effective in your teaching. As with any other instructional tool, use of technology must be carefully planned so that it is applicable and appropriately connects to the curriculum and lesson. Our message doesn't change, but how we present the message can change.

## TECHNOLOGY USE REQUIRES CHANGE

Adapting to using and incorporating technology into your instruction requires some change and preparation. Some Christian educators started teaching prior to the many recent advances in technology and may not have much, if any, experience using technology. But there's help! These teachers may have students in their classes, or have access to staff, that can assist them in understanding the different uses of technology.

Moving in the direction of adopting technology, Scott (2008) stated that an acceptance of the change requires a supportive environment. He further noted that someone in the environment must bear the responsibility for the kind of leadership that leads to effective technology implementation and change. The person in this role would provide for training, assistance, and support to teachers in the use of technology.

Many churches today have individuals in their congregations who are computer-savvy and have expertise in computers and information technology. Seek out and utilize these members of your congregation and their resources to help staff in the area of technology.

Training and support in how to use the various types of technology effectively are critical. This can be accomplished through workshops, trainings, courses, materials and resources, and one-on-one support. Part of the training should involve acquainting and familiarizing teachers with the types of technology available as well as giving them opportunities to practice using the various forms of technology with assistance, support, and feedback before being implemented in their classrooms.

## USING TECHNOLOGY IN LESSON PREPARATION AND INSTRUCTION

Technology is a tool. As such, it can enhance your instruction. It can be used in many ways in lesson preparation and instruction, and it can be used by both teachers and students. Use technology to encourage, motivate, inspire, teach, and inform students in a positive way that will enhance their spiritual growth. Always use technology in your instruction, in a purposeful and meaningful way, by somehow relating it to the lesson.

There are many technology tools available for teaching and learning. The following is a description of some of the most common uses of technology that Christian educators should become knowledgeable about and familiar with: they include use of the Internet, e-mail, text messaging, online conferencing, and multimedia presentations. As you plan your lesson, assess these resources to determine which ones best meet your instructional and classroom needs.

## THE INTERNET

One way to use technology as a part of your teaching ministry is through the use of the Internet. We have access today to a wealth of information instantly by merely clicking onto the Internet. The Internet allows people to communicate in various ways around the world. Besides, the Internet is a great tool for getting information and doing research. In order to connect to the Internet, you need a computer and connection to an Internet service provider.

Although you can find a vast amount of information on the Internet on just about any topic, it is important that you validate, verify, and evaluate the source and select your information carefully. Below are some of the many means through which you can obtain information on the Internet that can be helpful to you as a Christian educator:

- Instructional tools
- Resources
- Research
- Articles
- Maps
- Lesson activities
- Lesson plans
- Study sites
- Lessons
- Educational sites to help with your lesson
- Connection to software packages

In addition, you can create a classroom or Sunday school Web site that displays information about your class(es) and Sunday school in general. For example, you can put your lessons online, which is a great world outreach.

Many of the previously listed resources are free and can be downloaded from the Internet. A word of caution is in order, however: Always pay close attention to resources that are copyrighted and adhere to the pertinent copyright laws.

## E-MAIL AND CELL PHONES

Another way technology can be used in your teaching is through the use of e-mail and cell phones. These are ways of instant communication. For example, you can send, receive, and respond to messages instantly. Many people use these forms of technology daily as a convenient way to communicate and stay in touch. They have access to e-mail on their phones and computers. Some people also prefer text messaging as a way to send and receive short messages from their cell phones.

There are many ways you can use these tools to communicate with your students. For example, you can send a personal note to a student who was absent, a follow-up to a student, a prayer request, assignments, class announcements, reminders, class newsletters—and the list goes on in terms of ways in which these forms of technology can be used by Christian educators. It is also a way to communicate and share information with parents and other Sunday school staff members.

## ONLINE CONFERENCING

Online conferencing is another way to communicate and share information with others. Students and teachers can communicate and collaborate with each other, or teachers can communicate with other teachers through this form of technology. Participants can access online conferencing wherever they are and at any time from their computers via the Internet.

The ways you choose to use this tool are unlimited. It can be used to conduct live meetings or view presentations. You can answer questions that students may have before the next class or continue unfinished class discussions. You can plan, provide information, and share ideas. Students can work together on assignments and projects, and can train staff using this form of technology.

Popular online conferencing tools include:
- blogs
- Wikis
- Instant messenger
- podcasts
- Webcasting
- social networking
- Twitter

Below is a brief description of the aforementioned online conferencing tools.

### BLOGS

*Blogs* are two-way conversations hosted on independent Internet Web sites and sometimes referred to as "weblogs." They are a forum for dialogue and a way to get information to others. Blogs can be viewed by only a select group, or they can be set up to be viewed by the general public. Blog content includes various forms of information and can be used in a variety of ways. It can include questions, commentaries, feedback, comments, descriptions of events, and other material. It is a virtual arena where students can post their thoughts and ideas. The writer is referred to as a "blogger."

### WIKIS

*Wikis* are collaborative Web sites where users work on projects, documents, or assignments together.

## INSTANT MESSENGER
*Instant messaging* is a form of text-based communication. It is when two or more persons communicate over the Internet. They immediately acknowledge or reply to messages sent and received.

## PODCASTS
*Podcasting* is when you download digital media files to your computer, iPod, or mp3 player via the Web.

## WEBCASTING
*Webcasting* is a form of technology that delivers live audio or video events to your computer from the Internet.

## SOCIAL NETWORKING
*Social networking* is when there is a group of individuals who share common interests and activities. They communicate and share information online through e-mail and instant messaging.

## TWITTER
*Twitter* is a social networking service. It is another way to communicate and keep in touch with friends and others. Users send and read other users' short, text-based messages over the Internet. The messages are known as "tweets."

# MULTIMEDIA AND DIGITAL APPLICATIONS

Using technology in the form of multimedia applications means that you use more than one form of media in the same presentation. This way, students are learning from what they see and hear in a lively and interesting way, rather than from just the teacher's spoken words. When you integrate multimedia technology into your lesson, your classroom comes alive. Lessons become exciting! This is especially true today, when young people are so involved with technology and media. This is an excellent way to engage your students in the lesson.

You can create your own multimedia presentations or purchase them ready to go. Numerous Web sites can assist you in setting up multimedia presentations. PowerPoint, which is part of the Microsoft Office Suite, is a common form of multimedia and is an easy way to create a multimedia presentation. Additionally, training, online tutorials, and numerous Web sites can assist you in setting up a multimedia presentation.

By putting together the tools listed below, you can create a multimedia presentation. Multimedia resources include
- animations
- videos
- video clips
- graphics
- pictures
- charts
- visual imagery

- images
- audio
- sounds
- music
- CDs
- DVDs
- photos
- text
- PowerPoint presentations
- computers

As Christian educators, we should be open to learning about and using the most effective and efficient tools available to enhance our teaching ministries. Utilize the information presented in this chapter to explore the different options of technology available and determine the ones most appropriate. We also must be aware of the fact that technology changes quickly. In fact, it may change as quickly as every eighteen months or so. Our students are certainly aware of many of the changes. Christian educators must demonstrate their capacity for lifelong learning by utilizing new tools.

## **POINTS FOR DISCUSSION**

1. Discuss various ways you can use the Internet in your lesson preparation phase.

2. Why is it important to validate your online resources? Give an example.

3. If you were to use online conferencing, give an example of when and how you would use it.

4. Describe how you would use the technology of e-mail and cell phones to enhance your teaching ministry.

5. Design a plan that describes how you would use multimedia in your lesson presentation.

# Chapter 9

# Tips and Tools

This chapter is a presentation of some practical tips and tools that will add substance and excitement to your teaching and improve your effectiveness as a Christian educator.

## #1: CREATE A REFERENCE "TOOL BOX"

Effective teachers have a repertoire of resources they use to enhance their teaching. One such resource is a reference called a "Tool Box." To create a Tool Box, you will need a file box and index cards. In this box, you will organize and develop a file consisting of experiences that you have encountered in your Christian walk—both positive and negative. For instance, you may include a written description identifying events that document a time when God intervened and helped you through a particular or difficult situation, or perhaps other life-changing experiences. Be descriptive in relating the situations and outcomes. Label and place each event on a separate card.

Record special blessings, miracles, and lessons learned. In addition, identify, list, and categorize Scriptures that you use for particular situations and specific needs. After you have documented these events and Scriptures, categorize them, and put them in your Tool Box. You will have these resources to pull from to share with your students when similar situations, lessons, and experiences are addressed in your teaching, or when applicable to a particular lesson that you may be teaching. There may also be times when you need to reference them yourself.

It is good to share the experiences of others, but there is nothing like having your own personal testimony. As you begin to prepare your lessons, look for those personal life experiences that you have had that you can relate to the lesson. In other words, use every opportunity to connect biblical principles to everyday life experiences. Information shared from your Tool Box can bring hope, encouragement, help, inspiration, and revelation to your students.

Whether or not you choose to use the Tool Box idea, you need some personal experiences that you can share with your students. These experiences add validity and substance to your lessons and to your teaching as they reflect on the goodness and power of God. You need to know without a doubt from your own personal experiences that God "is able to do exceeding abundantly above all that we ask or think" (Ephesians 3:20, KJV).

## #2: CONSIDER JOURNALING

Keep a journal. This is a way to capture and express your thoughts, experiences, prayers, and ideas in writing. It is also a way to reflect on the lessons you have taught. It is a wonderful tool to log and document important information. Journaling can be used in many different ways for different reasons. You may keep several journals for different topics. You can collect and capture quotes, sayings, and wisdom notes and reference them in your teaching. Journals can be used to record prayer requests for others and prayers for yourself. In your prayer journaling, you want to make sure you monitor and document answered prayers.

## #3: RECOGNIZE AND ACKNOWLEDGE YOUR STRENGTHS AND WEAKNESSES

Christian educators are not perfect. They have flaws and inadequacies just like everybody else. To move forward and be used by God in the most effective way requires that you assess your strengths and weaknesses periodically. After identifying them, make a plan for improvement and making a change. The T-chart on the following page can help you through this process.

Just because you have some deficits in an area(s) does not mean that God cannot use you. He has used and continues to use individuals with flaws. The apostle Paul, in his writing, said, "Brethren, I count not myself to have apprehended: but this one thing I do, forgetting those things which are behind, and reaching forth unto those things which are before, I press toward the mark for the prize of the high calling of God in Christ Jesus" (Philippians 3:13-14, KJV). Like Paul, you must be willing to recognize your weaknesses, deficits, and mistakes, but, in doing so, have a desire to move forward. That's why as Christian educators we have to rely on God's help and power to move us from Point A to Point B.

God used Moses, who had a speech impediment; Paul, who had a thorn in the flesh; Peter, who had a temper; and David, who did some terrible things that he later regretted (but the Scripture says that he was a man after God's own heart). God used each of these men in a mighty and marvelous way. He can use you, too!

## Assess Your Strengths and Weaknesses
List your strengths and weaknesses.

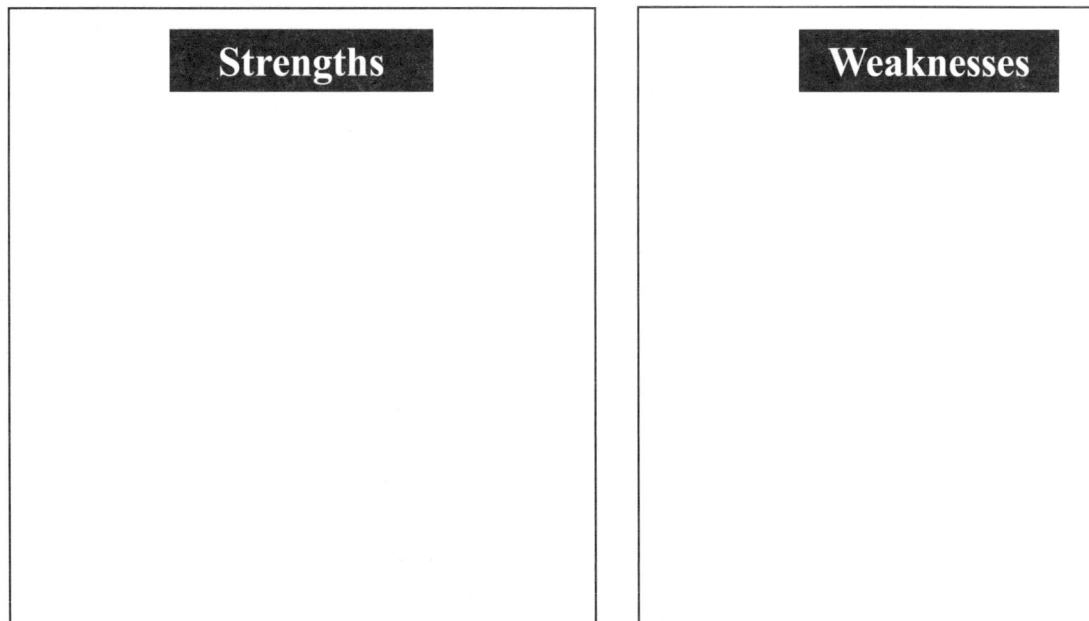

After assessing your strengths and weaknesses, determine an area(s) in the "Weaknesses" column in which you want to improve. Think about where you would like to be as a Christian educator in six months, one year, and five years. Not only do you want to think about where you want to be, but also you need to make a plan and determine what you need to do to get there. On the following page is a form that can help you accomplish this goal.

# Christian Educator Action Plan

Area of concern _____

Goal: _____

Benefits of achieving the goal: _____

How do I plan to achieve my goal? The answer(s) to this question will be your objective(s). Your action steps will be how you plan to get there.

|  |  |  |  |  |
|--|--|--|--|--|
|  |  |  |  |  |
|  |  |  |  |  |
|  |  |  |  |  |
|  |  |  |  |  |
|  |  |  |  |  |

Complete a separate form for each area in which you want to improve. Identify goals that address your target area(s) of concern. Give some prayer and thought to this process. Make sure your goals are practical, realistic, and manageable. Evaluate and assess your progress regularly.

God is our source and help. Without Him, "we are like a ship without a sail." When you are called to teach God's Word, He will equip and empower you to do the job. But we must recognize the areas in which we need help. God will give you what you need. With prayer, study, and preparation, He will help you communicate His Word most effectively to the students you are teaching. God will help you develop into an even greater teacher, the kind of teacher that He expects you to be.

## #4: DRESS FOR SUCCESS—YOUR APPEARANCE IS IMPORTANT!

How you look and present yourself to your students is very important. As a teacher, your appearance is very important. Your appearance is reflected in more than just how you look; it is also how you present yourself to your students. For instance, how do you look and present yourself when you stand before your students? Do you look happy, sad, pleasant, perplexed, miserable, depressed, or uncertain? Do your posture and voice display confidence, certainty, and boldness? Is your head up and are your shoulders straight? What kind of facial expressions are you displaying? Do you come to class complaining? Do your demeanor and personality change from week to week?

Come to class with a pleasant and positive attitude, geared up and ready to teach. Speak and teach with clarity, boldness, authority, assurance, and confidence. Look at your students when you talk to them. Look at them and give them your attention when they talk to you. Eye contact is very important in keeping the attention of the class.

- Smile.
- Be cheerful.
- Greet your students warmly as they enter your classroom.
- Be enthusiastic.
- Have a positive attitude.
- Be an encourager.

## #5: WATCH WHAT YOU SAY AND DO

Christian educators must be cognizant of their actions at all times. You must guard what you say and do because you are being watched more than you may realize. Your students are watching what you say and do. What kind of image are you reflecting? In most instances, you will be looked upon as an example and as a leader, and in many instances your students will follow and mimic your leadership and example.

What you say and what you do also contribute greatly to the environment of your class. Since you are the leader and the example of the class you teach, it is necessary that you live the life of your teaching. Again, your students are watching you beyond the classroom. They watch how you respond not only during your good times but during your down times as well. That is why Christian educators must seek to live godly lives daily.

## #6: HEALTHY TIPS FOR HEALTHY TEACHING

Preparing to teach God's Word not only requires spiritual preparation—as important as that is—but it also requires that we prepare ourselves physically, mentally, and emotionally. You can't study, prepare, and teach your lesson effectively if you are exhausted, emotionally drained, stressed, sick, and tired all of the time.

Recognizing this, we must take care of our bodies so that we can be used to the fullest in God's service of teaching. God expects us to be good stewards of our bodies. Our bodies are the "temple of God" (see 1 Corinthians 3:16). When you take care of your body, it adds to your mental clarity, your physical energy, and your overall health, which will enhance your ability to study, prepare, and teach more effectively.

The following are some things you can do to be more physically, emotionally, and mentally prepared to teach God's Word:

- Organize and plan your day.
- Watch your diet.
- Eat healthy foods.
- Exercise regularly.
- Get plenty of rest.
- Get an early handle on situations, events, and special occasions that can become stressful.
- Give yourself plenty of time to do what you have to do.
- Get organized.
- Set priorities.
- Plan ahead.
- Have schedules and "To-do" lists and use them.
- Plan some quiet time.
- Prioritize the number of events, functions, and meetings you attend.
- Learn to delegate.
- Monitor your schedule to avoid overload.

## MINIMIZE THE STRESS IN YOUR LIFE

Too much stress can have negative consequences on our bodies. In fact, stress can be detrimental to your health. You can minimize the stress in your life by doing all of the above, in addition to the following:

- Always have a "Plan B."
- Learn to say no.
- Live and enjoy one day at a time.
- Acknowledge God in all that you do.
- Learn to let things go (grudges, unforgiveness, disappointments, anger).

You now have the tools to become an effective Christian educator. Now, let's begin! Teach with passion, power, and purpose.

## **POINTS FOR DISCUSSION**

1. Using the chart on page 111, identify your strengths and weaknesses.

2. Identify an area of concern that you would like to begin working on. Write it as a goal and describe the benefits of achieving the goal.

3. Describe some things you can do to help you be more physically, emotionally, and mentally prepared to teach God's Word.

## TEACHER TRAINING

This section outlines a series of training modules developed from chapters in this book specifically for teacher training and professional development. The modules are designed to equip Christian educators with skills, knowledge, and practices to help them become more effective in teaching God's Word as they engage in a higher level of lesson preparation and planning to meet the needs of the students they teach. Each module addresses a variety of effective teaching practices that focus on application and implementation using andragogical (adult-centered) instructional learning principles as introduced by Malcolm Knowles (Knowles, 2004).

Training sessions can be conducted as part of your teacher training meetings, workshops, and other training venues. Trainings are organized in eight different modules. Each module lists a suggested training time; learning outcomes; teaching/instructional methods and activities; materials needed; as well as the instructional content addressed. Although a suggested timeline is listed for each module, trainings can be adapted for one or two hours, or half- or full-day sessions. They can be conducted weekly, monthly, or over the course of several weeks. Finally, the structure of the training allows you to select individual models for training as needed.

Training sessions are designed to be engaging, interactive, and applicable. Sessions are embedded with valuable information on effective teaching practices that can be immediately applied and implemented in teaching God's Word. Each session builds on the previous one and can be adapted to meet the needs of your teaching staff. Modules can be presented individually or in sequence. The following page displays the training topics at a glance. A table listing the handouts is provided at the end of the training modules section.

It is strongly suggested that you do the following:

- Develop PowerPoint® slides listing three or four bullet points to highlight information presented in each session.

- Give a brief overview at the beginning of each session describing what the module will address.

- Have norms for each session. Norms are the standards and attitudes that govern the behavior within a group.

- Begin each module with an opening and an introductory activity.

- Prepare all materials and handouts prior to training.

- Select appropriate instructional methods and activities as described in this book.

- Plan all activities with your participants in mind.

- Demonstrate with students how to complete the activities outlined in the modules.

- Make sessions interactive, engaging, and exciting.

- Bring a high level of enthusiasm to the training sessions with you.

Clearly communicate directions, frequently check student understanding, and monitor the timing of activities so that the training moves along and is completed in a timely manner. Move around the room while participants are engaged in activities to answer questions and to check for understanding. Watch the body language of your participants. End training sessions with a summary or some type of reflection activity. Thank participants for attending and participating. Have some form of evaluation for students to complete, and present a certificate for attendance. Do a self-assessment on how the training went. Provide date and time of next training if applicable. If a continuation session will follow, you may want to give an assignment in preparation for the next training.

May your teaching ministry be blessed to higher heights as a result of your utilizing the training modules!

## REFERENCE

Knowles, M. *The Adult Learner: The Definitive Classic in Adult Education and Human Resource Development,* 6th ed. Burlington, MA: Elsevier Inc., 2004.

# Appendix

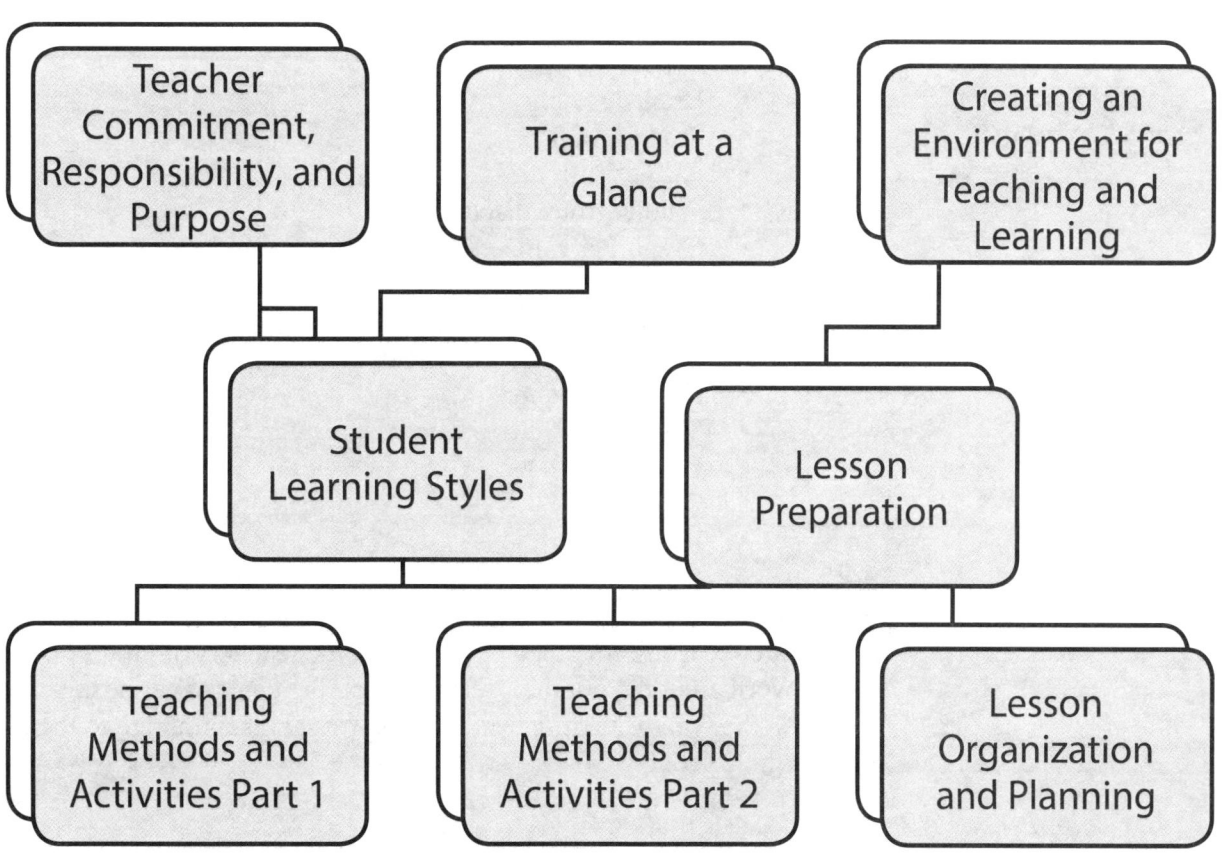

# Training Outline

| Module 1 | |
|---|---|
| This training module corresponds with chapter 1. | **Teacher Commitment, Responsibility, and Purpose** <br> *This session is designed for new and aspiring teachers.* |
| Estimated Time for Training | 2 hours |
| Learning Outcomes | During this module, participants will <br> 1. Reflect on their calling and personal commitment to teaching God's Word. <br> 2. Understand the impact they have on the lives of the students they teach. <br> 3. Describe what effective teachers do and what is involved in becoming an effective teacher. <br> 4. Describe essential qualities teachers must possess to be effective teachers. |
| Teaching/Instructional Methods/Activities | • Brainstorming <br> • Small group <br> • Partner activities <br> • Whole-group discussion <br> • Graphic organizers <br> • Reflections <br> • Discussion questions <br><br> • Flip-chart paper <br> • Markers <br> • Handout (1-1) <br> • Sticky notes <br> • Index cards |
| Materials | Begin the session by asking participants to list on sticky notes three reasons why they want to become teachers of God's Word and then put their responses on the chart paper posted on the wall. Categorize similar reasons and summarize to the whole group. |
| Instructional Content | *The module continues with the following instructional content:* <br><br> • The responsibility of teaching God's Word (pp. 1-3) <br><br> • Teacher influence on the lives of the students they teach (p. 4) |

|  |  |
|---|---|
|  | - Teacher commitment—What does that mean? What does it require (pp. 4-5)? Before your discussion, form small groups to discuss what commitment means and what participants think it requires. Groups should summarize their responses and post them on chart paper around the room. After the discussion, have participants revisit their lists and make changes or adjustments, as needed. Continue further discussion if needed.<br><br>- Teacher qualities and expectations (pp. 5-6)<br><br>- What effective teachers do (p. 6)<br><br>  Before the discussion, have participants complete a graphic organizer on what they think effective teachers do (Handout 1-1).<br><br>- Study Tools (p. 37). Bring examples to share.<br><br>- Form a panel comprised of three or four seasoned teachers to share their experiences in teaching God's Word. Instruct participants to write down on index cards one or two questions to ask panel members. Provide question cards to panel members prior to the panel discussion.<br><br>End with a summary of key points addressed during the session. |

## Training Outline

| **Module 2**<br>This training module corresponds with chapter 2. | **The Students You Teach** |
|---|---|
| Estimated Time for Training | 1 hour |
| Learning Outcomes | During this module, participants will<br>1. Understand why it is important to know about the age group they teach and how such knowledge is vital in their lesson planning and teaching.<br>2. Know the importance of building good student-teacher relationships and the impact it has on creating a more effective learning environment.<br>3. Share and generate ideas on how to learn about the students they teach. |

| | |
|---|---|
| Teaching/Instructional Methods/Activities | • Brainstorming<br>• Small group<br>• Partner activities<br>• Whole-group discussion<br>• Graphic organizers<br>• Reflection activities<br>• Discussion questions |
| Materials | • Flip-chart paper<br>• Markers<br>• Handouts (2-1, 2-2)<br>• Index cards<br>• Sticky notes |
| Instructional Content | Begin with a brief brainstorming activity. Ask participants to discuss with a partner "Why is it important to know about the students we teach?" Post the question on chart paper, a handout, or a PowerPoint® slide.<br><br>*The module continues with the following instructional content:*<br><br>• Discuss the importance of building relationships with the students you teach (p. 8).<br>• Have participants consider the needs, issues, and concerns of the students they teach, and list on graphic organizer: Effective Teachers (Handout 2-1).<br>• Discuss the importance and benefits of knowing the students you teach.<br>• Discuss different ways to learn about the students they teach and why this information is important (pp. 8-9). Assign participants to work with a partner or in small groups to generate creative ways to learn about the students they teach and ask them to share with the whole group.<br>• Give an overview of the characteristics and age-group differences of each age group (children, youth, and adults) and how these students learn best (pp. 13-15).<br>• Form small groups to discuss the characteristics of the age group participants teach.<br><br>Close with participants completing 3-2-1 Reflection Activity (Handout 2-2). |

**Training Outline**

| Module 3<br>This training module corresponds with chapter 3. | **Creating an Environment for Teaching and Learning** |
|---|---|
| Estimated Time for Training | 2 hours |
| Learning Outcomes | During this module, participants will<br>1. Identify key components that are needed to create an effective environment for teaching.<br>2. Learn how to assess the teaching environment and how to use the information gathered to make adjustments that allow for effective teaching to occur. |
| Teaching/Instructional Methods/Activities | • Brainstorming<br>• Small group<br>• Partner activities<br>• Graphic organizers<br>• Whole-group discussion<br>• Reflection activities<br>• Discussion questions |
| Materials | • Flip-chart paper<br>• Markers<br>• Handouts (3-1, 3-2)<br>• Index cards<br>• Sticky notes |
| Instructional Content | Begin this module by instructing students to write one word on an index card or sticky note that describes their classroom and share with a shoulder partner to get them thinking about their classroom environment.<br><br>*The module continues with the following instructional content:*<br>☐ Discuss the classroom environment (pp. 16-18) to include<br>    o Classroom climate<br>    o Teacher's role in setting the tone for the learning environment<br>    o Creating a positive learning environment<br>    o What it looks like<br>    o How to make it happen<br>    o Room appearance, organization, and arrangement<br>    o Setting up the environment to allow for student participation |

|  |  |
|---|---|
|  |    o Creating a learning environment for creative and effective teaching<br>• Have participants complete Environmental Classroom Checklist (Handout 3-1) and classroom section of the Classroom Environmental Analysis (Handout 3-2). Ask participants to identify and list what they can do to improve their teaching environment.<br><br>Close the session with a reflection activity (refer to p. 60). |

## Training Outline

| **Module 4**<br>This training module corresponds with chapters 4 and 9. | **Student Learning Styles** |
|---|---|
| Estimated Time for Training | 2-3 hours |
| Learning Outcomes | During this module, participants will<br>1. Understand the different ways students learn and what it means to the teacher learning process.<br>2. Assess and determine how they learn best.<br>3. Assess and determine their strengths and weaknesses, and make a plan for improvement and growth. |
| Teaching/Instructional Methods/Activities<br><br><br>Materials | • Small group<br>• Partner activities<br>• Questions<br>• K-W-L activity<br>• Handouts (4-1, 4-2, 4-3, 4-4)<br>• Flip-chart paper<br>• Markers |
| Instructional Content | Begin the module by asking participants to list what they know about student learning styles and what they want to know about student learning styles on the K-W-L Activity Sheet (Handout 4-1). Instruct participants to only complete the first two columns. Have them share their responses with a partner; then ask for responses from some of the participants. Let them know you will ask them to come back to this handout at the end of the session.<br><br>*The module continues with the following instructional content:*<br>• Discuss the three common learning styles: visual, auditory, and kinesthetic. Give a description and examples of each learning style (pp. 24-25). |

|  | • Assess the learning styles of the students you teach.
• Discuss the importance and benefits of designing lessons to incorporate and reflect different learning styles (p. 26).
• Have participants assess their own learning style by completing the Learning Styles Assessment (Handout 4-2) and What Is Your Learning Style? (Handout 4-3) to determine how they learn best and what it means to their teaching and learning.
• Instruct participants to assess their strengths and weaknesses as a Christian educator and identify one area of concern to begin working on immediately. Guide them through the Christian Educator Action Plan (Handout 4-4; p. 112) and give them time to complete it.

As a closing activity, instruct participants to complete the last column on the K-W-L sheet, "What I Learned," reflecting on what they learned during the session. |
|---|---|

## Training Outline

| **Module 5**<br>This training module corresponds with chapter 5. | Lesson Preparation |
|---|---|
| Estimated Time for Training | 4 hours |
| Learning Outcomes | During this module, participants will<br>1. Identify key components involved in lesson preparation.<br>2. Understand why it is important to plan lessons with their students in mind.<br>3. Know what study tools and resources are necessary as they study and prepare to teach God's Word. |
| Teaching/Instructional Methods/Activities | • Small group<br>• Partner activities<br>• Questions<br>• Whole-group discussion<br>• Jigsaw<br>• Round-robin activity |
| Materials | • Handouts (5-1, 5-2)<br>• Flip-chart paper<br>• Markers<br>• Index cards |

| Instructional Content | Begin the module by instructing participants to individually complete the following sentence stem: *Lesson preparation involves . . .* Assign small groups to work together to share, discuss, and come up with one sentence. Have each group read their sentence to the whole group. |
|---|---|
| | *The module continues with the following instructional content:*<br>• Discuss the components of effective lesson preparation and planning (p. 35).<br>• Review ABCD Teacher Preparation Plan (p. 36).<br>• Complete a jigsaw reading activity (Handout 5-2) on the ABCD Teacher Preparation Plan. Refer to page 48 for directions on how to use the jigsaw activity.<br>• Review lesson preparation tools (p. 37).<br>• Discuss key questions to consider before planning a lesson (p. 43).<br>• Discuss Lesson Preparation: Ten Key Questions to Ask (Handout 5-1). Instruct participants to work with a partner and complete this handout using a recent lesson taught. Hold a discussion on the implications of completing this handout when preparing to teach a lesson.<br><br>End with participants reflecting on what they learned and experienced during the session. Ask them to select a keyword or an idea that is significant to them. Then have them share their word or idea in small groups in a round-robin group activity (refer to p. 75 for instructions on how to complete the round-robin activity). |

Training Outline

| **Module 6**<br>This training module corresponds with chapter 7. | Lesson Organization and Planning |
|---|---|
| Estimated Time for Training | 6-8 hours, or four 2-hour sessions |
| Learning Outcomes | During this module, participants will<br>1. Learn how to structure the presentation format of a lesson (opening, body, closing).<br>2. Learn how to develop effective lessons that engage students in the learning process.<br>3. Practice writing lesson outcomes. |
| Teaching/Instructional Methods/Activities | • Small group<br>• Partner activities<br>• Jigsaw<br>• Graphic organizer |

| | |
|---|---|
| Materials | - Handouts (6-1, 6-2, 6-3)
- Flip-chart paper
- Markers |
| Instructional Content | Begin by asking participants to individually complete Handout 6-1 (T-Chart), Organization and Planning: What Is the Outcome with It and without It? Encourage participants to fill in several ideas. Hold a discussion with the whole group on their responses.

*The module continues with the following instructional content:*
- Discuss how effective planning prevents chaos and confusion (p. 80).
- Describe the three lesson presentation phases (p. 81).
- Discuss the importance of developing a plan for teaching (p. 82).
- Provide instruction on the steps to effective lesson planning.
    - Step 1: Writing Lesson Objectives/Outcomes (pp. 83-86). Jigsaw, page 84 (refer to page 48 for directions).
    Review Bloom's Taxonomy, a tool to use when writing objectives (Handout 6-2). Have participants practice writing lesson outcomes for each category listed in Bloom's Taxonomy, using an identified or familiar lesson. Discuss the importance of linking the lesson, objectives, and activities (pp. 84-91).
    - Step 2: Materials/Resources/Supplies (p. 87)
    - Step 3: Lesson Introduction/Opening—discuss introduction activities (pp. 89-90)
    - Step 4: Determining Teaching Methods and Procedures (p. 91)
    - Step 5: Lesson Conclusion/Closure (p. 94)
    - Step 6: Assignments for Next Week (p. 94)
    - Step 7: Follow-Up (p. 94)
    - Step 8: Assessment/Evaluation—checking for student understanding and application (pp. 91, 92, 94, 95)
- Discuss ways to obtain feedback from students (p. 95).
- Have teachers complete the Teacher Self-assessment (Handout 6-3), assessing the last lesson they taught.
- Have participants discuss in small groups what went well, what did not go so well, and what can be done differently next time.

End the session by having participants complete the 3-2-1 Reflection Sheet (Handout 2-2). |

Training Outline

| **Module 7** This training module corresponds with chapter 6. | Teaching Methods and Activities Part 1 |
|---|---|
| Estimated Time for Training | 6-8 hours, or two half days |
| Learning Outcomes | During this module, participants will<br>1. Identify what must be considered when selecting a teaching method.<br>2. Understand the impact of using more effective methods of instruction versus only using traditional methods.<br>3. Learn and practice different teaching methods that can be used in Bible teaching. |
| Teaching/Instructional Methods/Activities | • Think-pair-share<br>• Small group<br>• Jigsaw activity<br>• Partner activities<br>• Whole-group discussion<br>• Demonstration<br>• Oral presentations |
| Materials | • Handouts (7-1, 6-2)<br>• Flip-chart paper<br>• Markers |
| Instructional Content | Begin the module by having students complete a think-pair-share activity (Handout 7-1). Instruct participants to identify and list different methods Jesus used in His teaching. After sharing with a partner, ask participants to share with the whole group.<br><br>*The module continues with the following instructional content:*<br>• Teaching Involves More Than Telling (p. 46). Have participants jigsaw this section (refer to p. 48 for jigsaw instructions).<br>• Factors to Consider When Selecting a Method (p. 47)<br>• Making Smooth Transitions (p. 47)<br>• Traditional Versus More Effective Methods (pp. 48-49)<br>• Lecture (p. 51)<br>• Questions (pp. 52-53)<br>• Types of Questions (p. 53)<br>• Use Bloom's Taxonomy as a framework for writing questions (p. 52). Give participants time to practice writing questions for a lesson using Bloom's Taxonomy as a guide (pg. 85). Guide them through this process and provide feedback. |

|  | As a closing activity, have participants work in small groups and prepare a two- to three-minute presentation to be delivered to the whole group on one key topic addressed during the session. Assign a topic to each group. Encourage them to be creative in their presentations. |

**Training Outline**

| **Module 8**<br>This training module corresponds with chapter 6. | Teaching Methods and Activities Part 2 |
|---|---|
| Training Duration | 6-8 hours, or two half days |
| Learning Outcomes | During this module, participants will<br>1. Learn and practice different teaching methods that can be used in Bible teaching.<br>2. Identify when to use certain instructional methods and activities (before, during, and after instruction).<br>3. Develop a list of teaching aids to use to support instruction. |
| Teaching/Instructional Methods/Activities | • Small group<br>• Partner activities<br>• Whole-group discussion<br>• Demonstrations<br>• Oral presentations |
| Materials | • Flip-chart paper<br>• Markers<br>• T-chart |
| Instructional Content | Begin the session with the following question, "Why is it important to use different teaching methods when teaching a lesson?" Form small groups to discuss answers to the question. Provide opportunity for groups to share with the entire group.<br><br>*The module continues with the following instructional content:*<br>Use demonstrations in presenting the teaching methods and activities listed below. Engage participants in activities that will give them an opportunity to practice each of the teaching methods and activities presented. Encourage creativity.<br><br>• Think-pair-share<br>• K-W-L activities<br>• Reflection activities |

- Visual charts/graphic organizers
- Partner and small-group activities
- Brainstorming
- Round-robin
- Group discussion
- Class discussion
- Interviews
- Storytelling
- Debate

Assign participants to work in groups to practice using two or three instructional methods/activities with an identified lesson (either teacher- or student-selected). Give participants an opportunity to share their experience in using the various methods and activities with the whole group.

(**Note:** The methods and activities listed were selected by the author; however, instructors can select additional ones that are listed in chapter 6 to incorporate into the training.)

- Discuss teaching aids that support instruction (p. 78).
- Discuss key components of team teaching (p. 28).
  Have participants identify and discuss in small groups the pros and cons of team teaching. Responses can be recorded on a T-chart or on flip-chart paper. Allow groups to share their responses with the whole group. Summarize key points.

Close the session with participants sharing with the whole group key information they have learned and how they plan to apply it in their teaching.

# Handouts

**MODULE 1**
Graphic Organizer (Effective Teachers)
1-1

**MODULE 2**
Graphic Organizer (The Students You Teach)     2-1
3-2-1 Reflection Sheet     2-2

**MODULE 3**
Environmental Classroom Checklist     3-1
Classroom Environmental Analysis     3-2

**MODULE 4**
K-W-L     4-1
Learning Style Inventory     4-2
What Is Your Learning Style?     4-3
Christian Educator Action Plan     4-4

**MODULE 5**
Lesson Preparation: Ten Key Questions to Ask     5-1
Jigsaw Activity     5-2

**MODULE 6**
T-Chart     6-1
Bloom's Taxonomy     6-2
3-2-1 Reflection Sheet     2-2
Teacher Self-assessment     6-3

**MODULE 7**
Think-Pair-Share Activity     7-1
Bloom's Taxonomy     6-2

**MODULE 8**
There are no new handouts for this module.

**Handout 1-1**

## Graphic Organizer

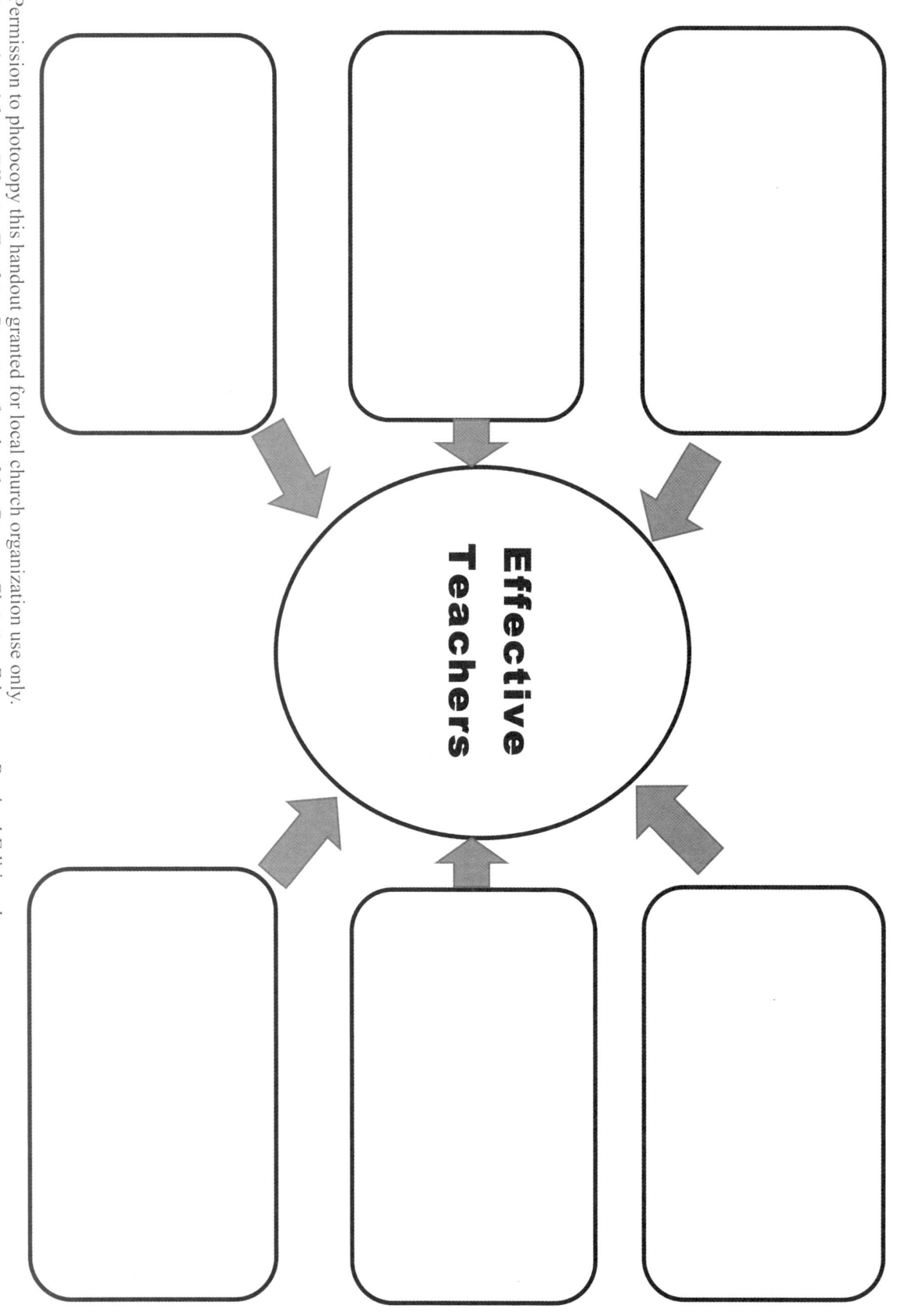

Permission to photocopy this handout granted for local church organization use only. Reproduced from *Effective Teaching Practices for the 21st Century Christian Educators*, Revised Edition, by Mary E. McConnell, Ph.D. Copyright © 2015 by Townsend Press.

Handout 2-1

# Graphic Organizer

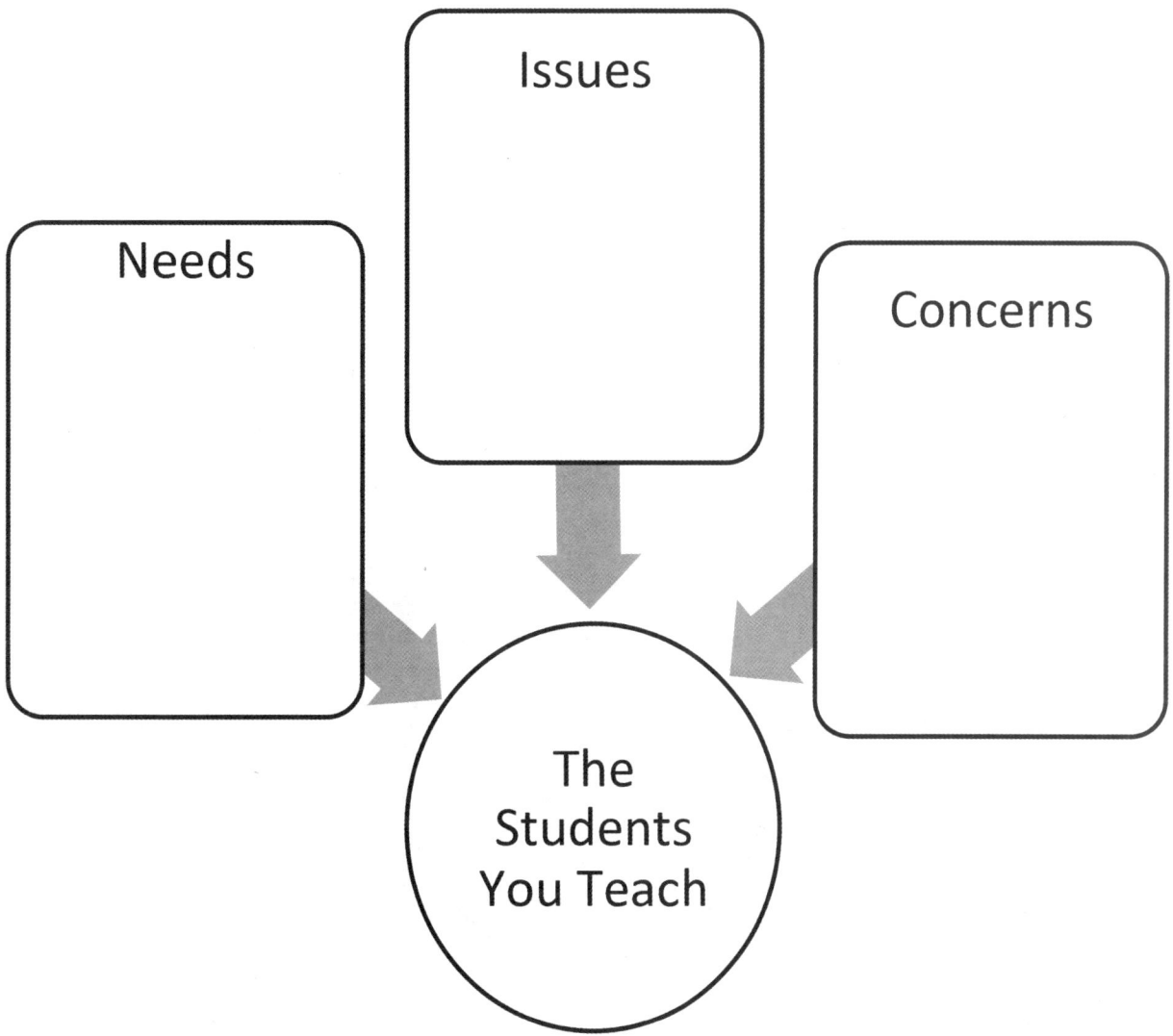

Permission to photocopy this handout granted for local church organization use only.
Reproduced from *Effective Teaching Practices for the 21st Century Christian Educators*, Revised Edition, by Mary E. McConnell, Ph.D. Copyright © 2015 by Townsend Press.

(Handout 2-1)

# Graphic Organizer

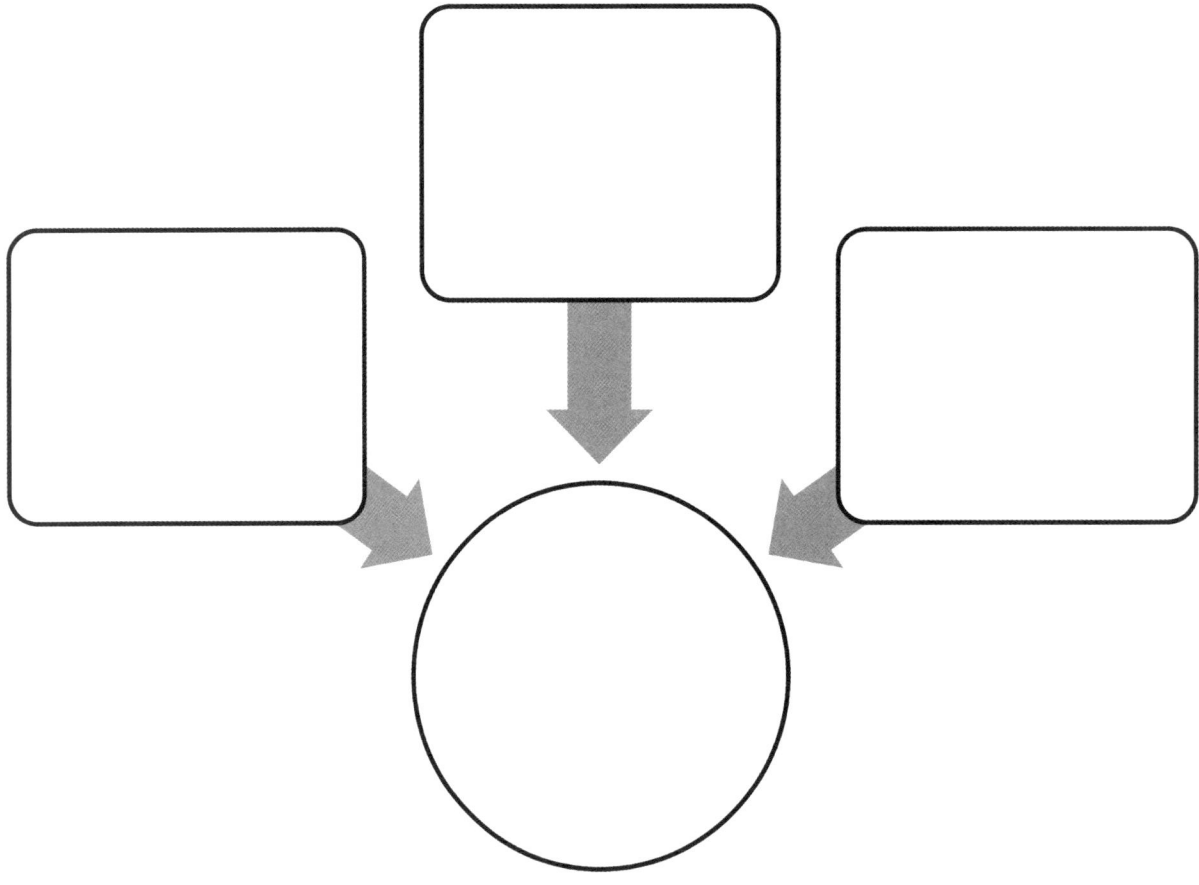

Permission to photocopy this handout granted for local church organization use only.
Reproduced from *Effective Teaching Practices for the 21st Century Christian Educators*, Revised Edition, by Mary E. McConnell, Ph.D. Copyright © 2015 by Townsend Press.

# Reflection from Today's Session

**3** things I learned or relearned

**2** things I will implement immediately

**1** thing I will do differently

Permission to photocopy this handout granted for local church organization use only.
Reproduced from *Effective Teaching Practices for the 21st Century Christian Educators*, Revised Edition, by Mary E. McConnell, Ph.D. Copyright © 2015 by Townsend Press.

Handout 3-1

# Environmental Classroom Checklist

Class:_____     Date:_____

Teacher(s):_____

|  | YES | NO |
|---|---|---|
| 1. Have you assessed your classroom environment lately? | | |
| 2. Do all of your students feel welcomed and accepted in your class? | | |
| 3. Is your classroom dull, or is it attractive? | | |
| 4. Do your students look forward to coming to your classroom? | | |
| 5. Are their ideas and suggestions welcomed? | | |
| 6. Do they get a chance to participate, or do you do all of the talking? | | |
| 7. Is your room set up in such a way that all students can be engaged in the lesson? | | |
| 8. Are there distractions? | | |
| 9. Is spiritual growth taking place in the lives of your students? | | |
| 10. Have you had new students join your class lately? | | |

Permission to photocopy this handout granted for local church organization use only.
Reproduced from *Effective Teaching Practices for the 21st Century Christian Educators*, Revised Edition, by Mary E. McConnell, Ph.D. Copyright © 2015 by Townsend Press.

Handout 3-2

# Classroom Environmental Analysis

Teacher(s): _____ Age Group: _____ Class: _____

Classroom Location: _____ Length of Class: _____ No. of Students in Class: _____

| Classroom Environment | Teacher Expectations |
|---|---|
| Describe your classroom setup and student seating arrangement: | What are your expectations for your students? |
| What is the atmosphere in your classroom like? | Describe what your class participation looks like. |
| Identify distracters: | How do you involve students in the lesson? |
| How many students do you typically have? | Do students have assigned responsibilities? |

Permission to photocopy this handout granted for local church organization use only. Reproduced from *Effective Teaching Practices for the 21st Century Christian Educators*, Revised Edition, by Mary E. McConnell, Ph.D. Copyright © 2015 by Townsend Press.

(Handout 3-2)

## Lesson Delivery

What instructional methods do you typically use?

What does your lesson presentation generally consist of?

What do you do to reach all of the students in your class?

## Materials

What instructional materials do you typically use?

What curriculum do you use?

What supplemental resources do you use when presenting the lesson?

*Permission to photocopy this handout granted for local church organization use only. Reproduced from Effective Teaching Practices for the 21st Century Christian Educators, Revised Edition, by Mary E. McConnell, Ph.D. Copyright © 2015 by Townsend Press.*

(Handout 3-2)

| Teacher Behaviors | Outside Assignments |
|---|---|
| What do you like about your class?<br><br>Is there anything you would change about the way you conduct your class?<br><br>What is your attitude toward your class? | What types of assignments are given and how often?<br><br>How do the students respond to the assignments given? |

Adapted from McConnell et al. (2000). *Functional behavioral assessment: A systematic process for assessment and intervention in general and special education classrooms.*

Permission to photocopy this handout granted for local church organization use only. Reproduced from *Effective Teaching Practices for the 21st Century Christian Educators*, Revised Edition, by Mary E. McConnell, Ph.D. Copyright © 2015 by Townsend Press.

Effective Teaching Practices for 21st Century Christian Educators

# K-W-L Activity

| What I Know | |
|---|---|
| **What I Want to Know** | |
| **What I Learned** | |

Permission to photocopy this handout granted for local church organization use only. Reproduced from *Effective Teaching Practices for the 21st Century Christian Educators*, Revised Edition, by Mary E. McConnell, Ph.D. Copyright © 2015 by Townsend Press.

Handout 4-2

# Learning Style Inventory

Name_____        Date_____

How do you learn best? This inventory helps you determine your learning style. Circle the numbers below that identify how you prefer to learn.

When learning, I prefer to
1. work with my hands.
2. talk to myself while reading a book.
3. hear things explained first.
4. move about and take frequent breaks.
5. watch a DVD or film.
6. experience it.
7. listen to a teacher's or someone's explanation.
8. listen to CDs, tapes, the radio, or recordings.
9. watch someone illustrate or demonstrate the information.
10. perform through simulations, games, or role-plays.
11. look at charts, maps, graphs, or pictures.

When studying something to remember it (memorization), I prefer to
12. say it to myself.
13. write it.
14. read it.
15. hear it.
16. do an activity to learn it.

When reading, I prefer to
17. underline, highlight, or circle important points and write notes in the margins.

Refer to the next page to determine your learning style.

Permission to photocopy this handout granted for local church organization use only.
Reproduced from *Effective Teaching Practices for the 21st Century Christian Educators*, Revised Edition, by Mary E. McConnell, Ph.D. Copyright © 2015 by Townsend Press.

**Handout 4-3**

# What Is Your Learning Style?

Place in the identified column the number preferences you circled identifying how you prefer to learn best. Then total the number of circles for each category. Based on the totals, determine your learning style preference.

| Auditory Learners | Visual Learners | Tactile/Kinesthetic Learners |
|---|---|---|
|  |  |  |
| Total | Total | Total |

Based on this learning style assessment, I tend to learn best using the _____ _____ learning-style modality.

Permission to photocopy this handout granted for local church organization use only.
Reproduced from *Effective Teaching Practices for the 21st Century Christian Educators*, Revised Edition, by Mary E. McConnell, Ph.D. Copyright © 2015 by Townsend Press.

**Handout 4-4**

# Christian Educator Action Plan

Area of concern: _____

Goal: _____

Benefits of achieving the goal: _____

How do I plan to achieve my goal? The answer(s) to this question will be your objective(s). Your action steps will be how you plan to get there.

| Objectives | Action Steps | Beginning Date | Ending Date | Objective Met |
|---|---|---|---|---|
|  |  |  |  |  |
|  |  |  |  |  |
|  |  |  |  |  |
|  |  |  |  |  |

Permission to photocopy this handout granted for local church organization use only. Reproduced from *Effective Teaching Practices for the 21st Century Christian Educators*, Revised Edition, by Mary E. McConnell, Ph.D. Copyright © 2015 by Townsend Press.

Effective Teaching Practices for 21st Century Christian Educators

Handout 5-1

# Lesson Preparation: Ten Key Questions to Ask

Lesson Title: _____ Date: _____

Lesson Scripture: _____

As you **read, study,** and **prepare** your lesson, ask **Who, What, When, Where, Why,** and **How** questions such as the ones listed below.

1. Who is speaking in this lesson? _____

2. Who is the author speaking to? _____

3. What time period was this lesson written? _____

4. What was going on at the time this lesson was written? _____
   _____
   _____

5. What are the main themes in this lesson? _____
   _____
   _____

6. Why did the author write this lesson? _____
   _____
   _____

7. What is the message in this lesson? _____
   _____
   _____

8. What happened as a result of the message in this lesson? _____
   _____
   _____

9. How does this lesson apply to today? _____
   _____
   _____

10. What does this lesson mean to me? _____
    _____
    _____

Permission to photocopy this handout granted for local church organization use only.
Reproduced from *Effective Teaching Practices for the 21st Century Christian Educators*, Revised Edition, by Mary E. McConnell, Ph.D. Copyright © 2015 by Townsend Press.

Handout 5-2
# Jigsaw Activity

Read and discuss your assigned section with your group. Write down important points from your topic or section.

## Important Points

1.

2.

3.

4.

5.

## Key Ideas from Others

## Summary

Permission to photocopy this handout granted for local church organization use only.
Reproduced from *Effective Teaching Practices for the 21st Century Christian Educators*, Revised Edition, by Mary E. McConnell, Ph.D. Copyright © 2015 by Townsend Press.

**Handout 6-1**

# T-Chart

## Organization and Planning: What Is the Outcome?

| Without It | With It |
|---|---|
|  |  |

Permission to photocopy this handout granted for local church organization use only. Reproduced from *Effective Teaching Practices for the 21st Century Christian Educators*, Revised Edition, by Mary E. McConnell, Ph.D. Copyright © 2015 by Townsend Press.

(Handout 6-1)

# Bloom's Taxonomy

| Category | Definition | Sample Action Verbs to use in writing objectives | Sample Question Starters |
|---|---|---|---|
| **Knowledge** | Recalling and reciting information learned | Write<br>Name/Recite<br>Identify<br>Recall<br>State<br>Define/Explain | What did Paul say about…?<br>List three…<br>How would you explain…?<br>Can you name…? |
| **Comprehension** | Basic level of understanding; the ability to grasp the meaning | Explain<br>Discuss<br>Summarize<br>Describe<br>Paraphrase<br>Compare/Contrast | How would you summarize…?<br>Describe what happened when…<br>Can you put it in your own words? |
| **Application** | Applying information/ knowledge to a new situation | Demonstrate<br>Show<br>Produce<br>Complete<br>Discover<br>Prepare<br>Share | What examples can you find in the lesson that supports…?<br>How would you apply what happened to…? |
| **Analysis** | Breaking down into parts | Categorize<br>Compare<br>Analyze<br>Examine<br>Classify<br>Discuss<br>Probe | What conclusions can you draw from this lesson?<br>If…had happened, then what might the end results have been? |
| **Synthesis** | Creating, making, doing something; stresses creative behaviors | Compose<br>Construct<br>Develop<br>Prepare<br>Compile<br>Create<br>Generalize | What would have happened if…?<br>Do you believe… and why?<br>What is a possible solution to…? |
| **Evaluation** | Making a judgment about something; contains elements of all of the other categories | Assess/Evaluate<br>Compare<br>Interpret<br>Judge<br>Recommend<br>Justify<br>Critique | How would you compare the people's actions then to today?<br>What do you think about? |

Permission to photocopy this handout granted for local church organization use only.
Reproduced from *Effective Teaching Practices for the 21st Century Christian Educators*, Revised Edition, by Mary E. McConnell, Ph.D. Copyright © 2015 by Townsend Press.

Handout 6-3

# SAMPLE TEACHER SELF-ASSESSMENT

1. My teaching methods were effective.
   **List an example:**
   _____
   _____
   _____

2. I was able to connect with and reach all of the students in my class.
   **List an example:**
   _____
   _____
   _____

3. Every student had an opportunity to participate in the lesson.
   **List an example:**
   _____
   _____
   _____

4. The lesson went the way I anticipated.
   **List an example:**
   _____
   _____
   _____

5. The lesson did not go the way I anticipated.
   **List an example:**
   _____
   _____
   _____

**Notes:**
_____
_____
_____
_____
_____
_____
_____

Permission to photocopy this handout granted for local church organization use only.
Reproduced from *Effective Teaching Practices for the 21st Century Christian Educators*, Revised Edition, by Mary E. McConnell, Ph.D. Copyright © 2015 by Townsend Press.

**Handout 7-1**

# Think-Pair-Share Activity Sheet

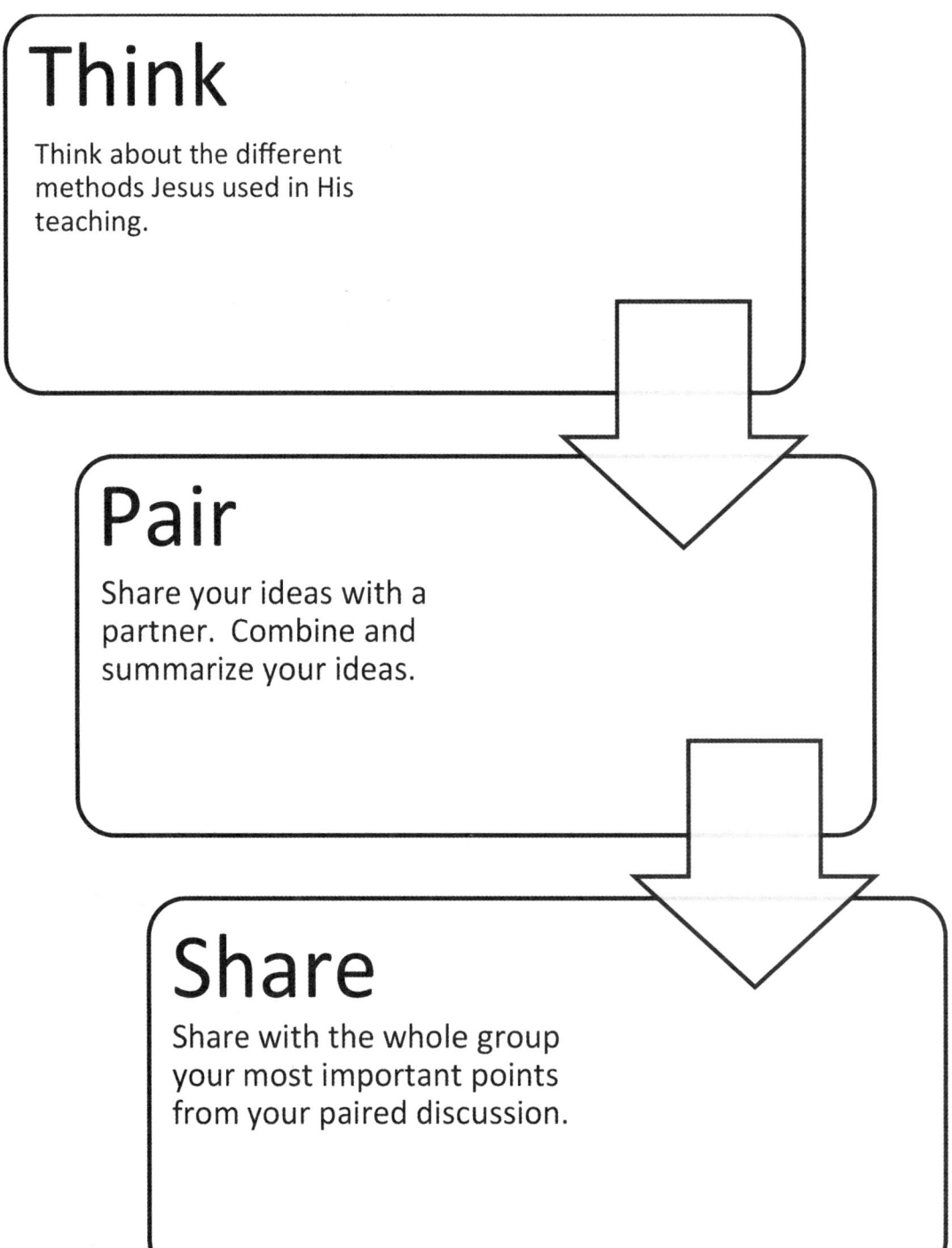

**Think**
Think about the different methods Jesus used in His teaching.

**Pair**
Share your ideas with a partner. Combine and summarize your ideas.

**Share**
Share with the whole group your most important points from your paired discussion.

Permission to photocopy this handout granted for local church organization use only.
Reproduced from *Effective Teaching Practices for the 21st Century Christian Educators*, Revised Edition, by Mary E. McConnell, Ph.D. Copyright © 2015 by Townsend Press.

(Handout 7-1)

# Think-Pair-Share Activity Sheet

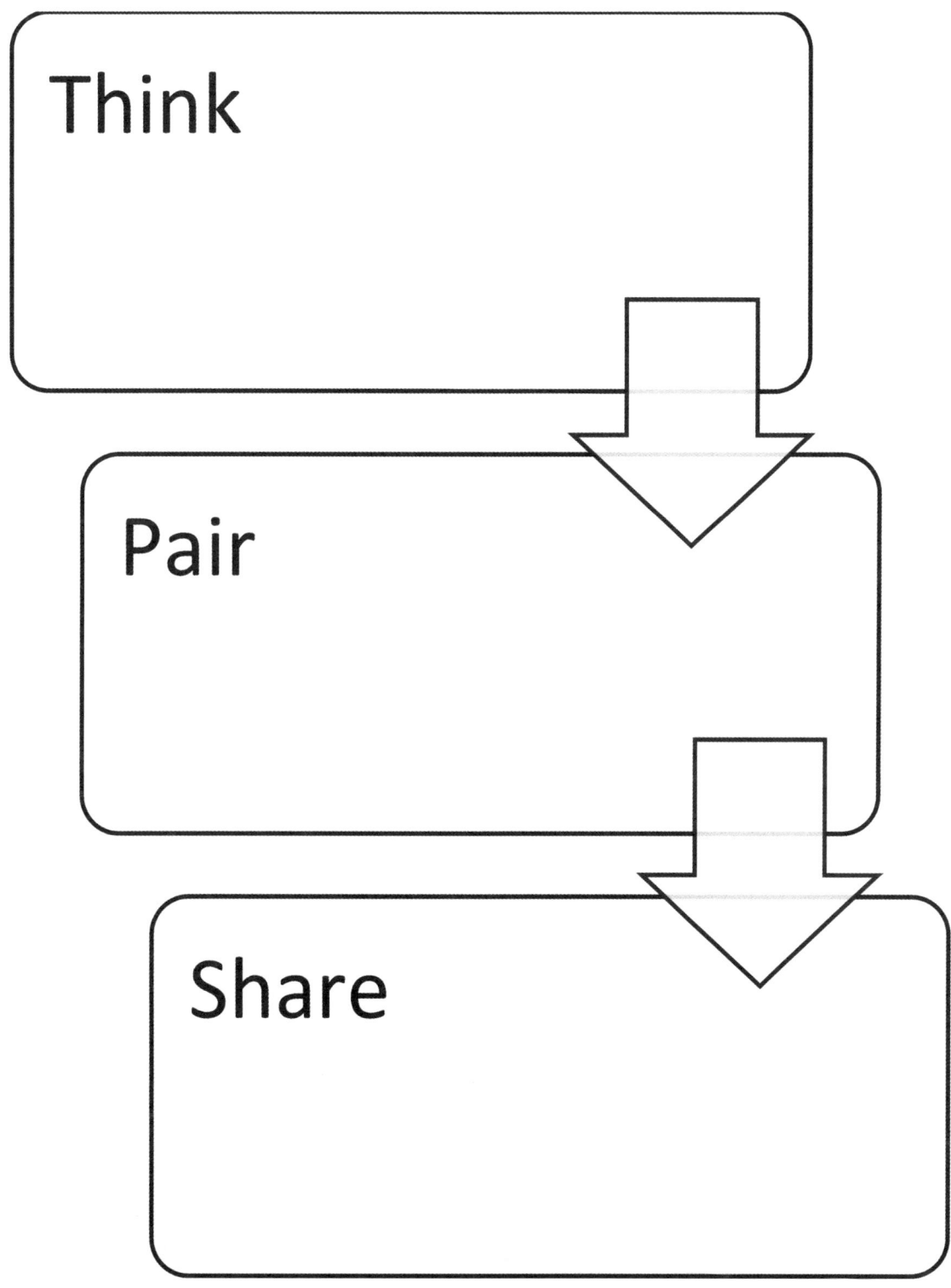

Permission to photocopy this handout granted for local church organization use only.
Reproduced from *Effective Teaching Practices for the 21st Century Christian Educators*, Revised Edition, by Mary E. McConnell, Ph.D. Copyright © 2015 by Townsend Press.

# References

Algozzine, B., J. Ysseldyke, & J. Elliott. *Strategies and Tactics for Effective Instruction*. Longmont, CO: Sopris West, 1997.

Bloom, B. S. *Taxonomy of Educational Objectives, Handbook I: The Cognitive Domain*. New York: David McKay Co., Inc., 1956.

Bolton, B. J., & C. T. Smith. *Creative Bible Learning for Children Grades 1-6*. Glendale, IL: CAG/L Publications, 1977.

Bull, K. S., & I. Land. *Developing Learning Centers Utilizing Bloom's Taxonomy for Secondary Students*. Paper Presentation, Bellingham, WA (ERIC Digest No. ED 262 493), 1985.

Campbell, L., & B. Campbell. *The Multiple Intelligence Series: Facilitator's Guide 1*. Alexandria, VA: ASCD, 1994.

Campbell, L., B. Campbell, & D. Dickinson. *Teaching & Learning through Multiple Intelligences*. Needham Heights, MA: Simon & Schuster, 1996.

Campus Crusade for Christ International. *Inductive Bible Study Method* (1997–2006). Retrieved March 26, 2008, from http://www.godsquad.com/discipleship/inductive.htm.

Chase, B. N. *Team Up for Better Teaching*. Cincinnati, OH: Standard Publishing, 1977.

Colson, H. P. *Preparing to Teach the Bible*. Nashville, TN: Convention Press, 1970.

Dobrovolny, J. *Learning Strategies* (2003). Retrieved July 29, 2008, from http://www.learningcircuits.org/2003/0ct2003/dobrovolny.htm.

Fister, S. L., & K. A. Kemp. *TGIF But What Will I Do on Monday?* Longmont, CO: Sopris West, 1996.

Forehand, M. *Bloom's Taxonomy: Original and Revised*. In M. Orey (Ed.), *Emerging Perspectives on Learning, Teaching, and Technology*. University of Georgia (2005). Retrieved August 18, 2008 from http://projects.coe.uga.edu/epltt/.

Galindo, I. *How to Be the Best Christian Study Group Leader*. Valley Forge, PA: Judson Press, 2006.

Gangel, K. *24 Ways to Improve Your Teaching*. Wheaton, IL: Victor Books, 1982.

Gardner, H. *Frames of Mind: The Theory of Multiple Intelligences*. New York: Basic Books, 1983.

Hall, T. *How to Be the Best Christian Educator You Can Be*. Chicago: Moody Press, 1986.

Hull, J. S. *Strategies for Educating African American Children*. Chicago: Urban Ministries, Inc., 2006.

Huitt, W. *Bloom et al.'s Taxonomy of the Cognitive Domain. Educational Psychology Interactive*. Valdosta, GA: Valdosta State University, 2004. Retrieved October 9, 2007, from http://chiron.valdosta.edu/whuitt/col/cogsys/bloom.html.

Krejeir, R. J. *Into Thy Word Ministries* (2006). Retrieved April 18, 2008, from www.intothyword.org.

LeFever, M. D. *Creative Teaching Methods*. Elgin, IL: David C. Cook Publishing Company, 1990.

Lieb, S. *How Adults Really Learn–Web Evangelism Guide* (2008). Retrieved April 16, 2008, from http://guide.gospelcom.net/resources/learning.php.

Marzano R. J., D. J. Pickering, & J. E. Pollock. *Classroom Instruction that Works*. Alexandria, VA: ASCD, 2001.

McConnell, M. E. "Strategies for Christian Education in the 21st Century." *The Christian Education Informer* 51, no. 3 (1998).

McConnell, M. E., C. J. Cox, D. Thomas, & P. B. Hilvitz. *Functional Assessment: A Systematic Process for Assessment and Intervention in General and Special Education Classrooms*. Denver, CO: Love Publishing Company, 2000.

McDaniel, E., & L. O. Richards. *You and Children*. Chicago: Moody Press, 1976.

Ormrod, J. E. *Educational Psychology Developing Learners* (3rd ed.). Columbus, OH: Merrill, 2000.

Pohl, M. *Bloom's (1956) Revised Taxonomy* (2000). Retrieved June 4, 2008, from http://eprentice.sdsu.edu/J03O/miles/Bloomtaxonomy(revised)1.htm.

Prenger, S. M. *Teaching for Inclusion: A Resource Book for Nu Faculty*. Teaching and Learning Center University of Nebraska–Lincoln, Lincoln, NE (ERIC Digest No. ED 446 575), 1999.

Rief, S. F., & J. A. Heimburge. *How to Reach & Teach All Students in the Inclusive Classroom*. West Nyack, NY: The Center for Applied Research in Education, 1996.

Richards, L. O. *You the Teacher*. Chicago: The Moody Bible Institute, 1978.

Rule, A. C., & L. H. Lord. *Activities for Differentiated Instruction Addressing All Levels of Bloom's Taxonomy and Eight Multiple Intelligences*. U.S. Department of Education (ERIC Digest No. ED 475 517), 2003.

Rushbuldt, R. E. *Basic Teacher Skills: Handbook for Church School Teachers*. Valley Forge, PA: Judson Press, 1981.

Schimmels, C. *Teaching that Works*. Cincinnati, OH: Standard Publishing, 1999.

Scott, M. "Educational Technology Leadership." *Technology and Learning* 28, no. 11 (2008).

Silver, H. F., R. W. Strong, & M. J. Perini. *So Each May Learn: Integrating Learning Styles and Multiple Intelligences*. Alexandria, VA: ASCD, 2000.

Sisemore, J. T. *Rejoice, You're a Christian Educator!* Nashville, TN: Broadman Press, 1977.

Stronge, J. H. *Qualities of Effective Teachers*. Alexandria, VA: ASCD, 2002.

VanSciver, J., & S. VanSciver. *Choosing Children's Sunday School Curriculum* (2007). Retrieved July 29, 2008, from www.religiousproductnews.com/archives/2007/apr/sundayschoolcurriculum.htm.

Web Evangelism Guide. *How Adults Really Learn* (2008). Retrieved April 16, 2008, from http://guide.gospelcom.net/resources/learning.php.

Winebrenner, S. *Strategies and Techniques Every Teacher Can Use to Motivate Struggling Students*. Minneapolis, MN: Free Spirit Publishing, 1996.